*Everyone must concede
that the kingdom of God
comes not through logical concepts
but through surprises.*

—Christoph Friedrich Blumhardt

Thy Kingdom Come

A Blumhardt Reader

edited by
VERNARD ELLER

WILLIAM B. EERDMANS PUBLISHING COMPANY
GRAND RAPIDS, MICHIGAN

Library of Congress Cataloging in Publication Data:

Eller, Vernard.
Thy kingdom come.

1. Theology — Addresses, essays, lectures.
I. Blumhardt, Johann Christoph, 1805-1880.
II. Blumhardt, Christoph, 1842-1919.   III. Title.
BR85.E48   230'.044   80-19328
ISBN 0-8028-3544-9

CONTENTS

Preface   ix

Introduction   xiii

part one   1

The Kingdom of God Is for Earth   3

The Living God   7

From Creation through Deterioration to Restoration   9

Jesus Christ   11

Redemption   18

   There Is Redemption   18

   The Redemption of the Body   18

   Political Redemption   20

   Social Redemption   22

   Redemption from Death   28

   Redemption from Evil   30

   Redemption from Law   31

   Redemption from Suffering   32

   Continuing Redemption   33

The Holy Spirit and His Gifts   34

The Living Christ   37

The Coming of Christ   40

The Spirit World   44

Fanaticism and Irrationality   47

Mankind   48

   God and Man—Humanity's Becoming Human   48

Of the Greatness, Freedom, and Glory of Man   49

No Nonentities   51

No One Bad or Godless   52

Love and Community   53

Godly Humanness   58

The New Revelation   60

The Bible   62

The Fall of Christendom   66

From the Spirit to the Letter   66

The Denial   66

From the Kingdom of God to "Religion"   67

The Church   71

Protestantism and Catholicism   73

The New Awakening and the Blumhardts'
Concept of Hope   75

How Does the Kingdom of God Come?   78

Gift and Task; Waiting and Working   78

The Little Flock   80

The People of God and the Service of God   83

The Zion of God   85

The Invisible Battlefield   86

Bad Boll, a Zion of God   87

The Human Vision   89

Work, Disappointment, and Fulfillment   91

Danger of Degeneracy   93

Being Quiet or Quietism?   93

Freedom or Formula?   94

Hearts or Heads?   96

Outlook and Task   98

Conclusion   100

part two   101

    The Name Jesus   103
    All Things New   111
    In the Return of Jesus Christ   115
    Wait for the Lord   118
    Standing Before the Son of Man   123
    God So Loved the World   130
    Who Forgives All Your Iniquity   138
    True Repentance   141
    The Poor   146
    God's Sheep   150
    Zion, the Mountain of Peace   154
    The Righteousness of God   157
    Wonders   161
    Nevertheless I Will Hold to Thee   165
    The Power of God   171
    The Right God   175

    Appendix   178

PREFACE

THE SUBJECT of my doctoral study was Søren Kierkegaard, the nineteenth-century Danish thinker. In the course of that research I came across Emil Brunner's testimony to the effect that the best predecessors of Neo-Orthodoxy were "two great figures of Pietism — Chr. Blumhardt, in Boll, and Kierkegaard." The strange pairing stuck in my mind: the name I had never heard along with the one heard all over the place. Were these two to be considered *equals*?

It was, then, in 1966 I discovered some of Blumhardt's work, namely, the 1963 Plough Publishing House translation of Lejeune's *Christoph Blumhardt and His Message*. Since that time it has been my magnificent obsession (well, *one* of my magnificent obsessions) to get more of the work of the Blumhardts — father and son — known in larger circles of Christian theologians and laity.

The Plough Publishing House is the publishing arm of that longstanding Christian community commonly known as the Bruderhof, officially as "The Society of Brothers," and more recently as "The Hutterian Society of Brothers." My interest in the Blumhardts immediately got me into contact with these dedicated and friendly people, resulting in two different visits to their headquarters and archives at Woodcrest, Rifton, New York.

Out of longstanding interest and through connections with descendants of the Blumhardts, the Bruderhof has been largely responsible for keeping the Blumhardt tradition alive in this country. These people regularly use readings from the Blumhardts in their worship and meditation. They are responsible for virtually all of the translation and publication of Blumhardt material in

English and hold the largest collection of Blumhardt materials outside Germany.

Gottlieben Blumhardt, daughter of Christoph Blumhardt, devoted the last years of her life to collecting the works of her father and grandfather. It was this effort that made possible the German publication of a great deal of Blumhardt material during the past decade.

It is too little to say that the Bruderhof has been *helpful* in connection with this book. Without the Bruderhof archives, Johann Christoph Arnold (the Plough publisher), and the anonymous members who did the first-draft translation of much of the material herein, this book simply would not have been possible. I want to take the opportunity to express my profound gratitude to the community and to all the individual members who have lent themselves to *our* magnificent obsession.

The search for a publisher to take on the book and competent translators to get the Blumhardts' German into English has been a long-drawn and many-directioned one. The publishers, of course, have now come down to one and the translators to four or five of us; but along the way, a whole host of well-wishers and moral-supporters did their bit to keep the obsession alive. For a while it almost amounted to the establishment of an underground Blumhardt society; my file of correspondence is several inches thick.

One sort of support came from several different book editors — none of whom were able to sell their houses on the book idea but who did give personal encouragement to the project. There *could* be enough Blumhardt books to have given one to each. I am sorry that did not happen; but I am grateful for their having made the big try.

Some of the people now to be named are since deceased, and others have moved from the institution with which they are here associated. Many of the contacts were made through the Bruderhof rather than directly with me. But one way or another, to one degree or another, there have been expressions of support from the following.

From Germany, Karl Barth (via a letter written by his secretary, Eberhard Busch); Eduard Heimann (a long-time colleague of Paul Tillich); Gottlieben Blumhardt (daughter of Christoph Blumhardt); Margrit Hönig (granddaughter of Christoph Blumhardt); and Christine Ragaz (daughter of the Swiss theologian, Leonhard Ragaz).

From this side of the ocean, Markus Barth (Pittsburgh Theological Seminary); James Smart (Union Theological Seminary); James Luther Adams (Harvard Divinity School), who also offered to speak for his deceased friend, Paul Tillich; Franklin Littell (Temple University); Harvey Cox (Harvard Divinity School); Martin Marty (University of Chicago Divinity School); and H. Martin Rumscheidt (Atlantic School of Theology).

Recommendations of this calibre convinced me that the project represented an essential contribution and thus kept me at it through the years. I am grateful to all these people.

Because of my own obvious inadequacy in the German language, I have had to have the help of those who could perform at least the first step toward an acceptable translation. These people will be named at the point in the book where they made their contributions; but here I want to take public notice of the time, effort, and skill they have given and express heartfelt gratitude for it.

Finally, I want to recognize and thank (without naming) all the relatives, colleagues, friends, and some new acquaintances who have constituted a general support group for the project and for me in the project. Among these certainly are to be included Eerdmans Publishing Company and all the people there.

— Vernard Eller
La Verne, CA
January 1980

INTRODUCTION

IN THIS introduction there are two things I want to do and one I do not want to do. The not-doing of the one will be the most difficult.

But, in the first place, no matter how sore the temptation, I am going to try not to do anything in the way of *introducing* the Blumhardts' thought — whether describing it, characterizing it, explaining it, or commenting upon it. Once start that and there would be no end. I prefer to devote the space to letting them introduce their thought for themselves — which is what this whole book is about.

Besides, these two are fully capable of introducing their own thought. Perhaps every word of theirs recorded here originated as oral discourse delivered informally before a *lay* audience. The Blumhardts may be the theologians who least need a third party to analyze and "explain" them. If their own words fail to inform, enlighten, or move the reader, there are no words of mine that could reverse the situation.

Besides attempting not to introduce the Blumhardts' thought, I intend to present a whole collection of facts purposed to show the sort of influence the Blumhardts have had upon modern Christian thought. The hope is that this will arouse within the reader the question, "Why have I not heard of them before?" thus exciting him to do something about it, namely, read the remainder of the book. Finally, then, I will offer brief biographical sketches of the two men.

The two Blumhardts, Johann Christoph (1805– 80) and Christoph Friedrich (1842– 1919), were father and son. Their careers — much more pastoral than theological in character — focused upon the son's succeeding his father as leader of what might be called a Christian retreat center that the father had established at Bad Boll in southwestern Germany. The thought of the two men shows enough continuity and agreement that it can be treated as one "theology."

We already have noted that Emil Brunner identified Christoph Blumhardt and Kierkegaard as the two greatest predecessors of the Neo-Orthodox movement. Karl Barth also said enough to indicate that he would agree with the opinion. And, independently, both Leonhard Ragaz and Theodor Haecker had made the same pairing and showed interest in it. Brunner's father had as much as been converted by the younger Blumhardt, which certainly made Emil's own relationship to Blumhardt much more than a sheerly intellectual one.

Eduard Thurneysen, Barth's long-time pastor-partner, visited Bad Boll and studied under Blumhardt as early as 1904. And it was he who subsequently introduced Barth to Bad Boll and to Blumhardt. In 1926, Thurneysen published a small book introducing Blumhardtian thought; and he quoted the Blumhardts at some length in his books on pastoral care. Over a period of thirty years, Barth wrote three different essays on the Blumhardts and gave them major notice both in *Church Dogmatics* and in other of his works. Barth's chosen touchstone for his own theology, "Jesus Is Victor," is a motto from Father Blumhardt. In Gerhard Sauter's doctoral study of the Blumhardts (the normative scholarly analysis of their thought), there is a major section entitled, "Considerations Regarding the Relationship of Christoph Blumhardt to Karl Barth."

James Luther Adams has testified to Paul Tillich's interest in what Adams calls "the religious-socialist element in Blumhardt" — although I think it would be fair to say that this social concern is about the only element of commonality between Blumhardt's theology and Tillich's.

When I was a seminary student, the book that set the direction of my understanding of scripture for time to come was Oscar Cullmann's *Christ and Time*. More than a decade later, upon discovering the Blumhardts, I was convinced I had found a fore-runner of the *Heilsgeschichte* (salvation-history) idea. When I met Cullmann, I put it to him whether he was familiar with the work of the Blumhardts and had been influenced by it. His face lit up like a Christmas tree. "Yes, yes, yes, yes, yes," he said.

I had not discovered that, in his published works, Dietrich Bonhoeffer ever mentioned the Blumhardts; but I had suspicions nevertheless. When the opportunity presented itself, I asked Eberhard Bethge, Bonhoeffer's confidant and biographer. He assured me that Bonhoeffer had been well familiar with Blumhardtian thought and strongly influenced by it. This is confirmed in Gerhard Sauter's study. Although it does not include a separate section on Bonhoeffer, that book, at a number of points in passing and in one passage of several pages, does rather conclusively demonstrate how several of Bonhoeffer's most important concepts tie back into the Blumhardts.

Even so, the fact that Gerhard Sauter is a recognized theologian in his own right and the fact that he has done this major study of the Blumhardts — these things have the effect of bringing the Blumhardtian influence directly into the present generation of German theologians with their "theology of hope," "political theology," and "liberation theology."

Karl Barth had called Blumhardt's a "theology of hope" long before Jürgen Moltmann was even born (in 1967, Moltmann published a book of that title to launch at least something of a movement). Moltmann is aware of the connection. As editor of the sourcebook, *The Beginnings of Dialectic Theology*, he chose one of Barth's Blumhardt essays for inclusion. And in personal conversation he was quick to confess his debt to the Blumhardts. There is no knowing how many more of the so-called "younger" German theologians would be ready to confess the same.

Finally, my own "best" theologians include not only Kierkegaard and the Blumhardts but also the contemporary French maverick, Jacques Ellul. Ellul has mentioned and quoted the Blumhardts a few times in his works. There are many of his ideas that *could* be attributed to Blumhardtian influences — although, most often, these probably came via Barth. Yet I did do an article showing the profound likenesses and convergences between Kierkegaard, the Blumhardts, and Ellul (with Malcolm Muggeridge thrown in as a fourth). Ellul himself accepted my interpretation wholeheartedly, demurring only that I had placed him "too high."

So the Blumhardtian heritage has been and even now is very much with us — mainly through the offices of the continental theologians with whom we have been involved. After this introduction already had been written, quite by accident I learned that the Blumhardts are better known among the Christians of Japan than among us, that there is more Blumhardt material in print in Japanese than in English. And that makes the question all the more poignant, "Why have we not heard of these Blumhardts before?"

Particularly is this so when we learn that, in Germany, Thurneysen's 1926 volume is circulating in a new edition; the 1887 biography of the elder Blumhardt has gone through at least twenty printings and is still available; the collected works of both Blumhardts are still in the bookstores. But on the other hand, in English, apart from a few books (such as those by Thurneysen and Barth, and a few on the history of Neo-Orthodoxy) which refer to and quote from the Blumhardts, virtually all of the Blumhardt material comes from the Plough Publishing House (the Bruderhof).

Heading that list is R. Lejeune's *Christoph Blumhardt and His Message*. Almost the first half of that book is given to Lejeune's introduction, the remainder of the volume presenting nineteen selected talks and sermons from the younger Blumhardt. Also important is *Action in Waiting*, a slight volume incorporating Barth's first essay on Blumhardt (1916) and one of Christoph Blumhardt's crucial sermons, "Joy in the Lord." Then there is a pocket-sized book, *Evening Prayers for Every Day of the Year*, compiled after his death from spontaneous prayers the younger Blumhardt used at Bad Boll. There is next a slim, 31-page paperback, *Now Is Eternity*, something of a random sampler of very brief "sayings" from both of the Blumhardts. And finally, there has just appeared a beautiful little 58-page paperback, *Thoughts About Children*, compiling material from both Blumhardts on the topic.

In addition to these from Plough, there is yet, from Thomas E. Lowe, Ltd., a 63-page paperback, *Blumhardt's Battle*. After a quite un-Blumhardtian introduction, this translates Father Blumhardt's official report to his Synod regarding his involvement with the case of demon possession of Gottlieben Dittus, one of his parishioners (which incident is recounted below).

"So why haven't we heard about the Blumhardts before?" Partly because so little material is available in English; and because what is available has come from small, private presses. "But why have other publishers failed to pick up on the Blumhardts?" My best guess in that regard is that, because the Blumhardt impact naturally came with the younger Blumhardt's maturity, death, and the generation of thinkers who continued the tradition from that point, and because that point itself coincided with the First World War, the war itself prevented the Blumhardt reputation from jumping either the English Channel or the Atlantic Ocean at the time it normally would have. Then, later was too late: why publish the works of the Blumhardts when no one knows who the Blumhardts are? — who would buy?

Now we will attempt to rectify that ignorance. The elder Blumhardt, Johann Christoph (1805 – 80), was educated for the Reformed ministry and, after a brief term as executive for a missionary society, became pastor in Möttlingen, an obscure village of Württemberg, southern Germany. His career was uneventful until, in 1842, he had to deal with one of his parishioners, a young woman, Gottlieben Dittus, who suffered some sort of severe nervous disorder and whose household was visited with strange psychic phenomena. Blumhardt concluded that the case was of a kind with those reported in the New Testament as demon possession.

After two months of pastoral care and reverent hesitation, discovering that he had no wisdom or power that could help, he and the girl prayed together: "Lord Jesus, help us. We have watched long enough what the devil does; now we want to see what the Lord Jesus can do." This prayer-battle continued for almost two years without change—the situation deteriorating, if anything.

Finally came the moment of crisis. At a point when Blumhardt's prayer and the girl's trouble were at a pitch, Gottlieben's sister (who had recently come under demonic attack herself) in a strange voice suddenly uttered the cry, "Jesus is Victor!"—and it was all over. Gottlieben later became a servant in the Blumhardt household and lived there the rest of her life; but she was never troubled again. Blumhardt understood the voice to be that of the demons who had just been conquered and expelled.

There is much in this story at which modern readers inevitably will look askance (as in the story to follow as well); but it must be said that both of the Blumhardts were solid, unflappable characters with nothing of the fanatic about them. In fact, rather than doing anything to encourage sensationalism or a personality cult centering in themselves, they regularly took deliberate steps to dampen such tendencies. Even so, very strange and wonderful things did take place.

Jesus' victory in the demented girl immediately triggered an in-breaking of kingdom power that transformed the entire village of Möttlingen and attracted people from miles around. The congregation experienced revival to a degree quite beyond even the dreams—let alone the actual accomplishments—of modern programs of church growth and renewal. There were many healings, conversions of some of the church's most determined opponents, and radical transformations of life and character. Marriages were saved, enemies were reconciled, there was an outpouring of evangelistic zeal and missionary fervor—all under the conviction that, because Jesus is victor, the kingdom of God has become a real possibility for life here and now.

As might be expected, this sort of goings-on at Möttlingen aroused the criticism of many of the church authorities. Blumhardt's vision of Christianity was larger than the church institution could manage. Thus, after a few more years at Möttlingen, the pressures toward churchly conformity became so restrictive that

Blumhardt gave up his pastorate and, for all intents and purposes, his formal connection with the Reformed Church. He moved a short distance away to Bad Boll, where he purchased a vacant resort hotel and made it into something of a retreat center, a place to which people could have recourse for periods of rest, meditation, study, and pastoral counsel — and a place where Blumhardt was free to operate according to God's leading.

He continued this ministry until his death in 1880, the testimony of his life perhaps best being summed up in a hymn with which he had been inspired at Möttlingen and which remained popular in Blumhardt circles:

> *Jesus is victorious Lord*
> *   Who conquers all his foes;*
> *Jesus 'tis unto whose feet*
> *   The whole wide world soon goes;*
> *Jesus 'tis who comes in might,*
> *   Leads us from darkness into light.*

Son Christoph was born at Möttlingen in 1842, at the very time his father was becoming involved in the struggle with Gottlieben's demons. As his father had done before him, he took university training pointing toward a Reformed pastorate. However, he became disillusioned with the church and theology and so decided simply to return home to Bad Boll and act as a helper there. Upon his father's death, then, he took over as housefather and continued the work until his own death in 1919.

In time, the younger Blumhardt became quite renowned as a mass evangelist and faith healer. But after a very successful "crusade" in Berlin in 1888, he drastically cut back both activities, saying, "I do not want to suggest that it is of little importance for God to heal the sick; actually, it now is happening more and more often — although very much in quiet. However, things should not be promoted as though God's kingdom consists in the healing of sick people. To be cleansed is more important than to be healed. It is more important to have a heart for *God's* cause, not to be chained to the world but be able to move for the kingdom of God."

Blumhardt's interest gradually took what could be called "a turn to the world," namely, a focus upon the great socio-economic issues of the day. Under the impetus of this concern Blumhardt chose, in a public and conspicuous way, to cast his lot with Democratic Socialism, the much maligned workers' movement that then was fighting tooth and nail for the rights of the working class. Although it brought upon his head the wrath of both the civil and ecclesiastical establishments, he addressed protest rallies, ran for office on the party slate, and was elected to a six-year term in the Württemberg legislature. He was asked to resign his ministerial status in the church.

Blumhardt began as a very active and energetic legislator, but as time passed he greatly curtailed this activity and bluntly declined to stand for a second term of office. Clearly, the pattern was of a piece with his earlier retreat from mass evangelism and faith healing.

Blumhardt's disillusionment with Democratic Socialism — i.e., with the party politics, not with the movement's purposes and ideals — and the even greater disillusionment which came toward the close of his life with the dark years of World War I — these brought him to a final position expressed in the dialectical motto: Wait and Hasten. His understanding was that the call of the Christian is still for him to give himself completely to the cause of the kingdom, to do everything in his power to help the world toward that goal. Yet, at the same time, a Christian must remain calm and patient, unperturbed even if his efforts show no signs of success, willing to wait for the Lord to bring the kingdom at his own pace and in his own way. And, according to Blumhardt, far from being *inactivity*, this sort of *waiting* is itself a very strong and creative action in the very *hastening* of the kingdom.

Blumhardt suffered a stroke in 1917 and died a peaceful death on August 2, 1919.

part one

LEONHARD RAGAZ (1868–1945) was a highly respected Swiss professor and theologian, one of the early contributors to dialectical theology, and a leader of the religious-socialism movement in Switzerland.

In 1922, he published a book of 321 pages, *Der Kampf um das Reich Gottes in Blumhardt, Vater und Sohn —und weiter!* The first 43 pages are an introduction to the Blumhardts and their thought (none of which we will use). The remainder is a presentation of their "message," the outline and headings of which become directly the outline and headings of our Part One, here following. Under each of these headings, Ragaz opened with his own description of and comment upon the Blumhardts' position (none of which we will use). Then he collected quotations and excerpts of the Blumhardts' own words on the topic. Although retaining all of Ragaz's headings, we have selected, to translate and present here, roughly half of the Blumhardt material Ragaz used.

Using Ragaz as compiler and editor, as it were, has given us inestimable advantages. (a) Ragaz presents a *comprehensive* and *ordered* (although not "systematic," which, regarding the Blumhardts, would be a wrongheaded impossibility) view of their thought which any amount of random reading in their talks and sermons could never provide. (b) Ragaz had access to the totality of the Blumhardt *corpus* in a way unsurpassed by anyone and unequalled by any contemporary, non-German scholars. (c) Ragaz knew the Blumhardts and their thought well enough and himself had sufficient theological expertise to make this an authoritative and dependable presentation of their "theology." (d) Ragaz was wise enough not to try to force their thought into the customary

1

categories and outlines of theology but to let the outline grow out of the Blumhardtian materials themselves. And finally, (e) Ragaz was a skilled enough editor that his selections do not read like a collection of "selections" but almost as though the Blumhardts had set out to write a presentation of their thought as a whole. In short, the Blumhardts nowhere expressed themselves as fully and as clearly as they do here with the help of Ragaz.

The *translation* of the Blumhardt material here presented (via Ragaz) is mine. However, I could not have managed it alone. A rough, first-draft translation for part of the material was provided by members of the Bruderhof (The Society of Brothers) who had been at work before I ever entered the picture. A second part was done recently by Professor William Willoughby, my colleague at the University of La Verne. And a third part was done some years ago by Lonna Whipple, then a La Verne College German major who had done her junior-year-abroad at Marburg University. To these people I tender my gratitude for their help. However, at the same time it must be said that, with their drafts beside me, I nevertheless worked directly from the Blumhardts' German (as given by Ragaz, of course). Thus, although they were most helpful, the translation is mine, and I must take full responsibility for it.

THE KINGDOM OF GOD IS FOR EARTH

There must be a new reality which is of the truth. It is not to be a new doctrine or law, not a new arrangement. The new truth to which we must listen is that which came in the person of the Son of Man himself, namely, that God is now creating a new reality on earth, a reality to come first among men but finally over all creation, so that the earth and the heavens are renewed. God is creating something new. A new history is starting. A new world is coming to earth.

Evil shall be defeated for all generations, and the good shall come into its rightful rule. That was the goal of the people of Israel, and for hundreds of years it was steadily pursued. The cause originally was an earthly one, not, as we Christians think, a heavenly one. It was the heavenly coming to reality upon earth; and to that extent it was earthly. It was earthly because it was a concern that the situation on earth become good and righteous, that God's name be hallowed on earth, that his kingdom come on earth and his will be done right here on earth. The earth is to manifest eternal life. We want to shine so brightly that heaven itself will become jealous of us.

Where in all the scriptures does God comfort man with a hereafter? The *earth* shall be filled with the glory of God. According to the Bible, that is the meaning of all the promises. Jesus, come in the flesh, what is his will? Of course, nothing other than the honor of his Father on earth. In his own person, through his advent, he put a seed *into the earth.* He would be the light of men; and those who were his he called "the light of the world" and "the salt of the earth." His purpose is the raising up of the earth and the generations of man out of the curse of sin and death toward the revelation of eternal life and glory.

Why else did he heal the sick and wake the dead? Why did he exalt the poor and hungry? Surely not in order to tell them that they would be blessed after death, but because the kingdom of God was near. Of course, God has a way out for those who, unfortunately, must suffer death; he gives them a refuge in the beyond. But shall this necessary comfort now be made the main thing? Shall the kingdom of God be denied for earth and perpetuated only in the kingdom of death, simply because God wants also to dry the tears of the dead? It is to discard the whole meaning of the Bible if one argues, "We have nothing to expect on earth; it must be abandoned as the home of man."

Truly, within the human structures of sin, we have no lasting home; we must seek what is coming. But what is it, then, that is coming? The revealing of an earth cleansed of sin and death. This is the homeland we seek. There is no other to be sought, because we do not have, and there cannot come to be, anything other than what God intended for us in the creation.

No *proper servant remains with his master solely for the wages* involved. If he realizes that he is of no use, he would rather leave and be poor. And no proper maid will stay just because of the pay. She wants to be of service. If there is nothing more to do, she is unhappy; even if she is paid, she no longer exists *as a maid*. And man, in the midst of creation, has the feeling that he is here for a purpose — not just for himself but for something else, something greater, something which has been lost.

Nevertheless, today people sit in the churches thinking mostly about *themselves*. Everyone sighs over himself, looks for something in himself and for himself — and doesn't himself know what it is. One would like to call out to them all: "People, forget *yourselves*! Think of *God's cause*. Start to do something for *it*. Don't be sorry for yourself; or at least be sorry that you have nothing to do but worry about your own petty concerns."

Our greatest lack is that we are of no use to the Lord; no wonder, then, that we go to ruin in spite of all our culture. Any person degenerates, even in a physical sense, if he is not acting as part of a body that has a higher purpose. But those who, in love and enthusiasm, work for something greater than themselves prosper, even regarding their physical well-being. And the race declines in its very life-values, both physical and spiritual, if, as people, there is nothing we are producing for the life of the earth, for creation, for God.

To believe in God is easy; but to believe that the world will become different — to do that one must be faithful unto death.

You know, the angels can't do much with "the blessed," because they seek only their own comfort in eternity and are no longer good for anything. One seats them in a comfortable chair and says, "There you are now; stay put." But when the kingdom of God is being fulfilled and many are pressing to enter, then there is really work and life among the angels. For the kingdom of God stands in a direct relationship to the earth; it lives *with* the earth.

Nothing will be revealed in the hereafter that is not already grounded here. God's goal is the here and now. It is here that the inheritance is to be received; and it comes as a work of *creation*, not of philosophy or theology.

Christians should take an objective view of the times. Instead, they want to experience everything subjectively within themselves and enjoy inner beatitude. Yet, these feelings have no permanency, and so they become disappointed. But when a person has his eye on a better future for *mankind*, then he gains a festival of the heart. A great confidence gives us strength for difficult times.

According to our customary false way of thinking, the kingdom of God must give way to our happiness. With many people the words of the Savior already have been altered to read: "Seek first your own blessedness, and all these things shall be added unto you." This is something very deceptive, although I know that for me to say so will rub many people the wrong way. They love *themselves*; and if only they know that they are safe, they don't much care about the rest of the world — or at most, only so much as to say to others, "See to it that *you* also get yourself saved, and then I will be happy!" With this little error, my friends, our fellowship with the Father is destroyed. We are like children always coming to our parents demanding candy, pop, and ice cream instead of being concerned about the wishes of our parents, honoring them with fidelity and hard work, in which case our food would come as a matter of course.

The goal of all God's effort is that finally he will be a God whom we will be able to see on earth, a God who will make the earth his footstool, where Jesus will be Lord over all men and where they, in him, once more will be integrated into God's creation.

THE LIVING GOD

What do I care about a God of the sort whose being must be demonstrated? The dear Lord came from heaven and *spoke*; had he not done so, even the philosophers could not have found him. Kant, Fichte, Hegel, Schelling — why, they would all still be heathen if he had not spoken his word on Mt. Sinai. I almost burst sometimes when our modern culture sets classical learning over the Bible. Why, everybody would still be ignorant were it not for the Bible and its God who there speaks upon earth.

God lets us meet him in Christ; and in the days of the apostles when there was talk of faith, of being true until death, everyone who belonged to the body of Christ knew what course his faithfulness would take. Something came over these people, something to which none of them had given thought and which none of them would have been able to explain. Suddenly they found themselves part of a history that proceeded of itself and in which such wonderful powers were discovered that the inevitable impression was: "These powers are stronger than the whole world."

In this situation people had a perfectly clear picture of what God is. There was no need to look up to heaven; the occurrences took place *on earth*; they were bound up with naming the name of Jesus.

In that regard, we ought not be ashamed frankly and openly to call our Christ "God," because, with only mental pictures of God, nothing gets started. Our Christ has become Yahweh; he stands upon earth and calls to us, "I am." And we need not make a big ceremony of it but simply fall before him, knowing in him

7

the living God, the Father in heaven. Then, once we have met him, we feel ourselves on solid ground which does not quake but from which the fountains of God's sovereignty burst forth to overwhelm us, as, in the final cataclysm, they shall overwhelm the whole world.

It may be that there is one error which poisons most of our thinking about God's kingdom. Prevailing very widely, this is the understanding that, in order for God's kingdom to come, it is sufficient that we finally and firmly establish and systematize the *doctrine*. This error works as a poison in that, from this perspective, certain doctrines and conventions soon become almost more important than God himself.

It has become clear to me that no single, dogmatic, fixed, and systematized doctrine will decide the issue of the kingdom; this only the living God himself will do.

As long as you believe sheerly as routine, things are not right. One cannot come drowsing into the kingdom of God. The cause must proceed with clarity and zest; the way must ever be made afresh by God. And therein is true grace demonstrated, that God hurries forth as the God who *acts*.

I tell you I cannot hold out for a single day unless from somewhere, either in myself or from afar, I have a report or am able to see that "Praise be, God is hurrying forward!" ... Thus we all should become enlightened in spirit so that we become clear about world events, so that we do not fall into religious confusion and other foolishness, so that we know what time it is, so that we have an inner sense about how to comport ourselves. "Shall I hurry? Shall I wait? Shall I do this? Shall I leave that?" In short, we need *light*.

8

FROM CREATION THROUGH
DETERIORATION TO RESTORATION

We are encompassed by a creation; and one piece of it is this ground under our feet. We go forth upon it; we live from it; we have a certain power over it; we are employed with it — and yet it nowhere comes completely right.

If one observes the morals, customs, viewpoints, and lives of all the world's peoples, he is amazed that, alongside the glorious appearance of nature's truth, mankind goes as if deranged. As the Chinese who bind a girl's feet are not satisfied until she is so crippled she can't walk, so do all the nations and peoples, be they Christian or heathen, right in the midst of the organism of truth which is creation, manage to make habitual falsifiers of themselves.

You must bear in mind, my friends, that we humans, even the best of us, are poor comrades to the great whole of creation. Something in us is twisted. Now, all of us were created in the image of God, an important part or — to put it pictorially — an important wheel in the great gearworks of creation. But on this wheel the cogs are all crooked and chipped; and the axle is bent. The human part doesn't work right; and the whole creation suffers in consequence. This is sin. Things don't run right with us men. There is much that is awry with every person in the world.

Is this creation to which our bodily life belongs simply to be cast aside? Or does there lie within it the embryo of eternity? There are many who see God's creation as of little value and its very loveliness as a sorry thing one would like to leave as soon as possible — preferably with a good kick. I am sad about that.

God did not create mere spirits for this corporeal world but bodies — which he has called his "image." Only through shattering travail can such a body come to be. And every person sees and experiences for himself that death is a judgment which makes him anxious even when he wants to be strong and convince himself that he can die tranquilly and be a spirit.

Men often attribute everything that happens in the world to God; but this is to do him an injustice. There are also works of man and of the devil. These do harm, whereas the works of God always do good — indeed, it is by this they are known. We are the ones responsible for so much that goes awry in the world. So lay off of my God, and don't say, "He's doing it!"

JESUS CHRIST

Jesus, who is the glory of God on earth, wants to help us become the same thing. In this man, God again shines forth. It is for a purpose, then, that he is here; he acts as God in the creation, among men. This is his work; consequently, he has eternal life and does not perish even though nailed upon the cross. Nothing, no possible situation, even the most disadvantageous you could conceive, can overcome this man, because he is here to accomplish something.

From him shines forth the Father of creation. And the creation feels that once more it has been given hope, as it were, because this man understands what needs to be done so that the things of God might again be brought into order and the ruined, wasted earth again be restored to him. I tell you, such is the Savior's first order of business. The Savior is, first of all, "for" God and only then "for" you. Bit by bit, man has turned things around and made the case appear as though the Savior had come only *for us*. Thus people use Jesus to flatter themselves; but this eventually can bring things to a pretty pass. I tell you, therefore, the Savior doesn't care about *us*, he doesn't even care about people as a whole — if they will not help *him*.

Without further ado he can put us all aside. Already he has begun to cut the threads; and — who knows how things will go? — it may happen that even the Christians will be left entirely on their own and have nothing more of a Savior.

He is the glory of God upon earth and the glory of man in heaven. Just as God was blotted out on earth, so also was man blotted out in heaven. Now Jesus comes as the one he is; and God lives upon earth. Then Jesus is again with the Father in heaven; and humanity lives there in him. Now before God there gleams something of the humanity which was dead; it is the glory of mankind in heaven before God through Jesus.

This is the man Jesus Christ: he is fixed in the creation where his true nature is grounded. As the creation is a work of God, so Jesus the Son is a work of God in the whole of creation. He is far above all angels and all powers of God that drive the world. The highest messengers of God, the life elements and life powers, serve him. He is in the creation, and it must go as he goes. One must understand this tremendous magnitude of Jesus Christ in order to believe that he still is able to help us men.

Jesus said, "I am the light of the world." That is true; nevertheless, it remains night as long as men are unaware of the fact and as long as Jesus is not known universally. We are in the night. That people have believed it to be day simply because Jesus was born, died, and rose again is the greatest error of Christendom. With that error we have been in the darkest night for nineteen hundred years, thinking that everything was complete and good.

But we must undertake great exertions if we are to be apostles of Jesus Christ. Our dead world must first be given light. Then it will be day. All people, all consciousness in heaven, on earth, and under the earth must know that Jesus bears all things and that he, as the glory of the sovereign God, as Son, rules the things of this world. Then it will be day; and then redemption will rush over all heights and into all depths.

One person we know through whom things moved as they should; he is called Jesus Christ. And thus it is that light has again been given to creation. Then why do you wonder at the fact that Jesus has bread for four or five thousand people? It amazes us; but he is simply a true man again, and that is why the powers of the world are subservient to him. Or why are you surprised that when he touches a sick person healing takes place? He is a true man. Things go as they should through him, under the oversight of God. He is the image of God, the Son of God. This makes him a blessing and constitutes a power which also makes others blessed if only they come within his reach. Even people who in themselves are perverted and godless, if only they press to him, are touched by something of his true spirit so that something comes true in them as well.

As long as it depends upon the perceptions merely of the eyes of reason, that understanding which is represented by research into the advent of Christ shall stand opposed to Christ's life in the will of God. So many people write "lives of Jesus" and seek to establish grounds for "the historical appearance of Christ"; and then they despair over the fact that we have such scant records in this regard. Neither the Gospel accounts nor the works of other authors of the time serve to satisfy the lust for the confirmation of this human history of Jesus.

The apostles and prophets don't even bother to give us the year of Christ's birth. Neither are they concerned to prove to the world the historicity of his singular life, the facts about his birth and the resurrection following his death on the cross. For the truth does not lie in the rationally verifiable history but in a life — a life which, out of an unpretentious and derided history, breaks forth as the life of God, while history according to the flesh is left behind as a useless shell.

The man whom you seek is not here (Mark 16:6), but the God-man remains and brings to people life and light. In this and that there may be contradictions in the reports godly people have handed down from those who knew Christ in the beginning, in what must be taken as *outward* history. It is little wonder if, where all sorts of people worked together in great enthusiasm, imperfect things got mixed in with the perfect; it is ever so with us humans. Also, after the Lord Jesus had given it into the care of the people, his history would have been passed along and elaborated. Yet, against this the Apostle Paul says, "I no longer know Jesus after the flesh" (2 Cor. 5:16). He does not intend to say that Jesus had not lived historically but that the outward history has fallen away and the life of God remains.

When the Spirit of God moves in a person who is seeking proof of God, that Spirit makes his appearance in the life of men actually upon earth and does not allow himself to be shunted into secondary matters. For the Spirit knows that the very crux of all truth lies in the kingdom of God — there rather than in the history of man according to the flesh, which shall disappear. A true history of man's life is in process of fulfillment, bound up with God, even though presently developing under the husks of an unfulfilled relationship. The Spirit knows that *this* life history is not that of tradition or historical research but of God himself entering the scene. Thus, after the history of mankind has been lost, the *life* of mankind still will be known, because, from beginning to end, it has been represented in the life of God himself.

Humanity indeed has its history. We can learn it — and we also can learn much *from* it. But this is not the history that truly brings joy to our hearts. The joy of human history is not so great that we would not gladly give it up. But there is also a history made up of experiences which are not confined to man himself but which are informed by something of the divine. That which is human must be touched by the divine.

When we read of the singular experiences of men of God from Abraham to Jesus and the apostles — let us admit it openly — they make us angry. What wouldn't people give if they could take Jesus without having to take in the bargain other events that are, humanly speaking, unexplainable? And to top it all off, in the resurrection Christ is raised to heaven. How unsettling this report is to all those who would like to make this dear man the founder of their religion — if only he had not said things or had things said about him that must make cultured people uncul-turedly ashamed.

How can those who still have faith in science imagine that a man dies and is buried and then later comes back and now lives beyond death? It is as if death were something one could just strip off, something one could come through without losing his physical existence but — quite the contrary — with the physical body transfigured. Yet all the experiences of the people of God point in this direction; and it is in these experiences, and not in the doctrines that follow from them, that the seeds of God's kingdom are found. The doctrines do not lead to experiences, but experience leads to doctrine; and for better or for worse, it is back to experience we must go if we would see the kingdom of God.

When Jesus came into our company, it was day. . . .

The whole history of humanity pivots, one might say, upon the works of Jesus. All that has come to pass since — the good and the evil, the bright and the dark — everything turns upon these works of Jesus which are directed toward the future of humanity.

It is something like the first beginning, about which, respecting our earth, it is so beautifully and significantly said: " 'Let there be light'; and there was light." From that moment on, there was nothing that could stop it. The earth had light, and from that light came everything else — all life, all aspects of life, all the perfecting of life. Everything, down to the deepest depths of the earth, even the coal mines, comes into being through the light. But what a development it all went through! There was much stirring of dust and mire, much destruction, much horror, much abomination — a fearful development — until finally there came out of the earth that which we enjoy today.

In like manner, a kind of light is given in Jesus. It is directed particularly toward man and, to begin with, toward only relatively few men. But whether shining upon many or few, the power of the Spirit's light calls people out to strive for a high purpose and not be satisfied with baseness; This light has appeared and even now shines forth. This light of the Spirit which has been implanted in humanity produces the greatest development, has the greatest power of revolution and advance for mankind, right up to the present day. A great deal of dust has been raised, the hideousness of man has been uncovered, because sin and brutality and vulgarity had to have their day. The history of Christendom following the coming of the light is a horror to behold and study. But what of that? . . .

It is so obvious in human history: there comes a time when something is born; and then things stand still and nobody follows up. There have been developments, and beginnings have been made, which we have failed to recognize. No one can comprehend the mere three years of Jesus' ministry as being the occasion of the greatest revolution ever to occur in human society. The rise of empires and nations, wars, battles, and victories — these are no "events," no "creations." In comparison to the high calling that is mankind's, all the empires of earth fade to nothing — as do all differences of race and language, all enmity, all hostility and arrogance between man and man. In the light of the creation that has come to us in Jesus Christ, all these things dissolve; nothing of them remains to be found. But that which does remain, which truly is of value for us — that has the permanence of eternity.

It *must yet come to pass that we will not simply hold fast to an* ancient confession of faith but out of a new experience be able to call to one another: "He is risen indeed! He lives among us! He takes the reins in hand and leads his people, leads them all the way to his death, that, in the death of the flesh, his resurrection and his life might be exalted in mankind to the eternal praise and glory of God."

For this cause is Jesus Christ risen from the dead: so that in him it can be seen that God will bring forth even *our* lives out of death and will take everything into his own hands once more. Therefore, we should die with Christ so that we also can be awakened and so that whatever *should* live will then be able to live fully and beautifully and gloriously.

The *Lord Jesus stands humanly very near to us; I do not know my* best friend as well as I know the Savior. I can't get inside my best friend; it is possible that there is within him that which is not quite trustworthy. But as far away as the Savior is from us, we still are so well-acquainted with him through the scriptures that he is, as it were, transparent to us. With the writings of a Cicero it is not so; though a person read Cicero as he will, he does not thereby see into his heart. Likewise with a Plato, a Socrates, a Virgil, all the noblest spirits — however beautifully they have written, they still do not become our friends. But the Savior comes in such a way that each person can be his friend. One has only to make his acquaintance; then everything comes of itself.

REDEMPTION

THERE IS REDEMPTION

When, as often happens, a person recites some sad case to me, some fate of life before which I shudder, I cannot simply say, "Accept your fate!" No, I say, "Be patient; the matter will be resolved — very surely it will be resolved."

Don't comfort yourself with that sort of Christianity which today practices the art of decking out every distress and wrapping everything in phrases to the effect that whatever happens is good. Don't accept such comfort; but seek with me people who stand before God and say, "Dear Father in heaven, we are not worthy to be called your children — but oh, that you once could use us as your hired servants!"

THE REDEMPTION OF THE BODY

The Spirit must embody itself. It must enter into our earthly life; it must happen that deity be born in flesh so that it can overcome this earthly world. God is active Spirit only when he gets something of our material underfoot; before that, he is mere idea. The Spirit would govern life.

It is a divine-natural law that body and soul hang together; and whoever would work on one part must take the other into consideration as well. Whoever would divide body and soul may be said to commit murder.

It seems to be the first concern of the human spirit that the body quickly become well; whereas, in silence the soul should thank God that, in its illness, the body had more rest than in its health — indeed, that it again feels more life and power than it did in healthy days. But many people become almost angry over such a consolation; they are so unaccustomed to being still and considering their lives that they forcibly push themselves back into the turbulence of activity. Yet precisely in this way do they stand in the way of their own health at the very moment God would put them under spiritual restraint, because he does not want them given over to destruction.

Harm to the body is the judgment upon man's drivenness of spirit. Wretchedness and darkening of the soul are judgments upon the vagabond life of the spirit. Therefore, it is important that every sick person who knows Christ should not make it his first impatient wish to become well. . . . [Rather,] he should first hold back his spirit and tame its wildness so that, through the person's own will, Christ can truly receive him and immediately bind him to God and his truth. That is to say, seek first the kingdom of God and his righteousness, and then body *and* soul will become healthy.

Being healthy is, to God, the same as being righteous. A healthy body, no matter how normal it may be, is not healthy in God's sight if it is dragging around in unrighteousness. In this way, stings of death press in by the thousands; and before they have outward effect, a body which appears healthy to us can be sick from head to foot, sick unto death. Righteousness is our health; and the first point of righteousness is that we allow ourselves to be bound by God so that our spirit no longer desires its own freedom.

As long as our spiritual piety does not present itself as true for the body, as right for the body, as freeing the body for God — as long as this piety is not free of human customs, insofar as these are perverted and out of harmony with divine laws — so long we remain only pious cripples. We must learn to be genuine creations of God through which life can stream out in all directions, as is the intention for all creation.

Therefore, we do not pray, "Do miracles," but rather "Let things go the way of truth." God should do miracles — but only when they are an aspect of the spiritual rectification of mankind. There must be a ground for them, a ground in the kingdom of God renewing and enlightening us from the divine side. It is *from this base* that miracles should take place; and then — yea, then — we shall shout aloud for joy, when, from within, things get set right. But at that point, *outward* miracles can disappear. ... I do not wish to see a single miracle in anyone that is not the consequence of that person's inner rectification.

POLITICAL REDEMPTION

Only revelation brings progress; and that is what makes it so important that finally revelation come into the body politic. That would be a real step forward for the world, because until now it has not happened. God has not yet truly entered into the history of the nations. There are only more and more human histories — as, for example, the Boer War. Only after such an incident can the Spirit of God give more light to individuals, Boers as well as Englishmen, so that they can see further. Yet, through revelation, enlightenment also must come into politics.

In several respects these are threatening times; and it is necessary that we keep faith and, in particular, that we not accept the belief that war or anything of the sort would improve our situation. Although it is heard among us, this word is only a form of despair which itself contributes greatly to the chances of war. God will look into such talk. There is absolutely no justification for war; and we can dare to trust his almighty arm even when that seems a very risky thing to do. We can believe that he will bring peace and, under any circumstances, send signs and wonders from heaven to help us. We need no swords or cannon. We should live and let live. So have mercy upon us, O Lord our God, that finally, finally, thou wilt create the kingdom of peace which thou hast promised.

Anyone with eyes in his head can see that in Europe nothing could be more sensible than efforts for peace. Whoever would speak a word against peace today is making a mistake. True, there is still a certain political atmosphere which has been cooked up, as it were. For centuries now a kind of lust for war has been working itself into the flesh and blood of Europeans and other peoples. This war-lust reigns within some sectors of the population; but stable people know nothing of it. Nevertheless, they let themselves too easily become enthused about it, because in the back of their minds still sleeps the idea, "There must be wars."

To this very day, in the political world there are certain questions for which we can find no solution except the sword. But it is scandalous to think that there should be no other solution than knocking one another around to see who is the more fortunate (one hardly can say "more powerful," because there are thousands of instances in which the more powerful have gone under). . . .

Whoever can think of it, should think once of how shriveled we are in a political sense. This great, round earth with its peoples, what an unconfined playground it could be for a genuine humanity, and how small we have made it in dividing up ourselves as tigers and lambs, fox and geese — with, naturally, the fox gobbling down the geese. On this earth, things go according to particular rules of animal life, and the life of the Spirit is not to be found.

Of course, thought cannot go too far in this direction before we come upon a word which is very much forbidden today. Yet there is something to be said for it. I will state it right out: "Anarchy!" Regarding the inhabitants of earth, a certain freedom, a veritable rulelessness, would almost be better than this nailed-up-tight business which as much as turns individual peoples into herds of animals closed to every great thought. . . .

Man is here to make progress; and if he wants peace he must also help bring it about — on his own ground, in his own way, seeking to bring it onto the scene. Mere talking and wishing that it would come of itself is of no value. Thus, everyone who wants peace must undertake peace, must be a man of peace.

And this in particular is what God would have us do now, out of respect for his eternal truth and righteousness. This is *our* calling; and who knows whether we are not the strongest ones in the present situation? I would not belittle those who strive for peace out of other considerations — out of sympathy, humanitarianism, and the like — but I do not believe that such efforts carry much power. However, there is a particular, invincible power in our efforts: as God wills, as the eternal truth wills, so *our* will is for peace; *our* will is that the peoples become changed and this terrible European history come to an end. . . .

If anyone remains stuck in the history we have had until now and thinks to find a solution there, he is a terribly small person. . . . Yet it is already something worthwhile if in these matters even a few people open their eyes to what is righteous, eternal, and true and thus make a firm resolution, "There must be a change!" To that degree, they are able to rise above the history of their time. And this will not have been done in vain; on the contrary, it will lead toward what we call the kingdom of God.

SOCIAL REDEMPTION

Is *Social Democracy that which rightly should be demanded? Or is* it rather — because it so energetically pursues "the state of the future" — that which, as so many assume, should by all means be opposed by every citizen and churchman?

A person must indeed be blind if he cannot see that, during the entire century since the French Revolution, there have arisen movements of ever increasing consequence directed toward a new ordering of society. Where is there a country that has not been agitated by Socialistic ideas? It is *one* impulse, *one* forward-striving spirit, that seeks this new social order. No one can avoid this movement. Church and state must grant people freedom in this regard. We have lived in a century of revolution and rapid change and are living in the midst of radical movements — and this is in accord with the will of God!

Notice how much our ways of looking at things have changed already! Who wonders today at the fact that every citizen demands political rights and receives them in ever greater degree? Who now is surprised when equal justice is demanded for all, both high and low? Is there anyone who wants to reintroduce slavery and indentured service? Or who would do away with representative government? These are genuinely new ways of looking at things.

In previous centuries, people who demanded the rights of freedom were simply brought to justice and exterminated. And now, when Socialism sets up the goal that every person have an equal right *to bread*, that matters of ownership be so arranged that neither money nor property but the life of man become the highest value, why should that be seen as a reprehensible, revolutionary demand? It is clear to me that it lies within the Spirit of Jesus Christ, that the course of these events leads toward his goal, and that there is bound to be revolution until that goal is reached. Resistance will be of no avail, because it is God's will that all men in every respect should be regarded equal and that they, rather than being plagued by the earth, should be blessed creatures of God.

That this struggle of the oppressed classes has not always gone pleasantly and that many imperfect things have been thought and done does not discountenance me. The basis of the movement, the energetic will, and the spiritual creativity of the goal are enough for me, so that I can feel myself an ally — and that, indeed, in the Spirit of Jesus Christ who had led me all along. . . .

But, you say, the Social Democrats want bloody revolution, illegal overthrow of the existing order, and general chaos. Now I say simply, that is not true. Many people have a horror of every revolution, because the French Revolution and the revolutionary movements which followed it were of a bloody nature. Yet the Reformation of the sixteenth century was even bloodier; why then do we not hate the Reformation? Because it, at least to some extent, brought *religious* freedom? Why then do we hate the revolutions of the eighteenth century? Is it because they helped people toward *political* freedom? The latter seem to me indispensable to the former. The bloodshed of the Reformation pains me just as much as the bloodshed of the Revolution; but I must take both in the bargain and in both see progress toward the freedom of humanity. Why don't we have a general horror of the bloodletting of times both past and present instead of a national prejudice that wants to ignore blood? Indeed, the whole world history is one long, revolutionary stream of blood. . . .

But people say, "Christ kept his distance from all such revolutionary ideas, having in view only the spiritual uplift of mankind." Yet, when he looked upon the temple of the Jews, when he came in touch with the false gods of nationalism and culture which stand opposed to the kingdom of God, he gave warning about the greatest sort of overthrow. "Not one stone shall remain standing upon another" is what he said about the proud national shrine of the Jews; and he saw destruction fast coming upon the capitalistic social system of that time.

He considered that the immediate result of his advent would be the greatest of revolutions; and he warned his disciples that things would be very violent. Of course, he went on to say that this was not the true end. At the very end, things shall proceed without violence. The Son of Man, the Man of Men, will come as a bolt of lightning lighting up the whole world. That suggests that God's thought and will shall drive universally and with power into human hearts, creating the people that God would have. And at that point we will be ready for a new heaven and a new earth.

However, if we were to bring together all the words of Jesus and the apostles dealing with the final purpose of human history, we would soon discover that, in spirit, Jesus concerns himself with the political and social situation, that his kingdom could not come or even be conceived apart from the overthrow of the established order. And he thought of this overthrow in essentially violent terms.

Nevertheless, this does not imply that, as followers of Jesus, we are to do deeds of violence. We are not to be bloody revolutionaries but to be filled with peace and power as we endure through the entire process, having our eyes fixed on the final goal of peace. Yet this end-state cannot come without the most shattering of overthrows. Like the whip which Jesus wielded in the temple at Jerusalem, there is still a whip to be wielded upon the whole unrighteous nature of humanity — "a day that shall burn like an oven," as the prophet Malachi said. And even if the judgment begins in the household of God, I will rejoice.

Even so, the Socialist movement is like a fiery sign from heaven warning of the coming judgment. And if Christian society is faced with a judgment, rather than becoming proud, let it consider well what truth there is in that which mounts the attack.

Yes, greed is the root of all evil! And it puzzles me that this truth is not more sharply felt. The truth is that our generation is perishing in its acquiring of money and its desire for money. Today nothing stands more high and holy in our eyes than speculation about money. Even among the wealthiest, many suffer from this burden; they take part in self-serving works of charity and yet are unable to be of real help to the miserable. True help will be brought only by the Christ of the all-encompassing End.

And now an organization arises, born out of bitterest need, and struggles toward this end, toward redemption from this world of money, this time of gold. And who would prevent me from giving this organization a hand in the name of Christ? Who will blame me for declaring the truth of those people's clear witness that we are on a downhill road, of their hope that in spite of all our present decadence we are coming to a better time, a time in which it will truly be said, "Peace on earth," a time giving birth to those who understand what life and salvation mean? Such is the goal of God's kingdom on earth, of the God who is a redeemer for all humanity.*

---

*Because Ragaz's personal predilection was to back Democratic Socialism even more fully than Blumhardt had ever done, he chose to give us only this one statement on the subject. However, if we are to get the total picture of Blumhardt's thought, we need also to hear these words spoken *after* his somewhat disillusioning experience with the party and as party spokesman in the Württemberg legislature. They are recorded in R. Lejeune's *Christoph Blumhardt and His Message*, p. 73:

"[Potentially, Democratic Socialism can] *further the thoughts of Jesus in the life of the nations more than any other movement.*"

"*In the social movement there lies an all-embracing concern for the* pure human life; quite generally the concern that men be helped. This has been accepted by the broad ranks of the people and is an echo of God's will that all men be helped."

"[Christendom] *has never expressed so conclusively this principle,* which lies in Jesus."

"*The social movement as we see it today still belongs to the world* which will pass. It does not contain the fellowship of men as it will one day come through God's Spirit. Too strong a defense of prevailing opinions has a flavor which is disturbing to the pure service of God."

"*The attempt to carry my idea of God into earthly things cannot* take root at a time when men are filled with the hope that they and they alone can create a blissful humanity. Now they first have to run aground on the rock of earthly things, in order to grasp the higher things."

Plainly, Blumhardt does not want to be understood as retracting what he said in the Ragaz quotation; we are not called upon to choose one Blumhardt over the other, the earlier over the later or vice versa. What the later Blumhardt did was to introduce a corrective (which may even have been implicit in the earlier statement). The truth, then, is to be found by holding the two positions in tension, letting each correct the other.

Thus, Christians must be open to perceive the hand of God even in those purely secular socio-political movements whose goals are *compatible* with the gospel picture of the kingdom of God. And once perceiving God's hand, we are, of course, under some obligation openly to welcome and support it. However, the later Blumhardt tells us, we dare never *give ourselves to* any socio-political movement as though it *were* the coming of the kingdom or an *equivalent* of that kingdom. No, Christian support of any and all such movements must ever include an element of "eschatological reserve," the freedom to criticize and even withdraw when, inevitably, anti-kingdom aspects of the movement show themselves. But it is quite possible to see Blumhardt as being right, as making a true Christian witness, both in joining and, later, in withdrawing from Democratic Socialism.

His total position, then, offers an essential corrective both to those Christians who want to forego all participation in the socio-political world and to those — such as certain proponents of Liberation Theology — who commit themselves so completely to particular party programs that, in the name of the gospel, they are willing even to give their blessing to revolutionary violence.
— V. E.

The will of God came forth in Jesus' coming forth upon earth. And what is he? He is the friend of men and of human society. And in a very particular way he holds society by what might be called its lowest part — by the miserable, the despised, the poor, by the masses of mankind who go through life unnoticed — this is where Jesus takes hold with a firm hand. . . .

No one else, even to the present day, no one who has not come from God *could* take upon himself this mass of mankind. A person representing only education, or only science and philosophy, or only human love and mercy, he would not come to these people. He would always think, "Oh, *them*; they are not important!" It is when he would meet a distinguished person, an honored one, somebody righteous, he would think, "Yes, it is with him I must join."

If anyone wants to found a party or amount to something, he seeks friends in the upper echelons of society. But the highest spirits, even the highest angels, cannot do what Jesus can. We put our hope in the professors or the exalted spirits of various sorts. We pin our hope on the highest heights of heaven; and Jesus places his hope in the proletariat, the outcasts, people whom kings and caesars ignore, with whom they dally as with playthings of the mighty — yet that is where Jesus sees the beginning of renewal. Will we follow him in this? It is just here that we must confess Jesus, that is, wholeheartedly press forward — for Jesus is *there*.

T*o my last breath I will fight for the sinners, the miserable, the* unwanted. And my great joy will be when I, to all that is high, can make clear what rottenness lies in "highness." And to my own house I would like to repeat every day, "Stay with the lowly!" And if we often seem to be a respectable social group, we should be ashamed that we are so respectable. Would to God we respectable people were all pushed into the corner and that those in rags would sit here! We would be a thousand times happier in so proclaiming such a Jesus. Yet the lowly ones must also come in.

REDEMPTION FROM DEATH

T*he hope of resurrection is an aspect of our longing for God's* kingdom; and the abolition of death is undeniably an element of the kingdom of God. Anyone who does not have the courage to accept this in all earnestness and give himself to the fight against death, he, we rightly can say, ought not be called a disciple of Jesus. ... All the words and works of God in Christ breathe the abolition of death.

This is the great triumph of the resurrection of Christ: people are born, people who already live. But those who live in sin and death are born again; and in them something new is revealed through the tremendous power of Christ Jesus. ... Acts of resurrection take place, new men arise, and here and there new people step forth so that one has to say, "There is a person in whom something new has been born."

I ask you, "Friends, from where does humanity draw its life? From where does Christianity draw its life?" We can answer with certainty: From those in whom the resurrection of Christ has repeated itself, those of whom it truly is said, "He who believes in me, though he die, yet shall he live, and whoever lives and believes in me shall never die" (John 11:25 – 26).

It is through those in whom Christ has become the resurrection and the life, through those who have become victorious in faith so that they trample the power of this world underfoot in the strength of eternity, which is the rule and power of Christ — it is through these people that the world endures even today. In them lives Jesus, the one risen from the dead. In them he rules and in them is victor. In them he is grace, is the light of the world. In them he will be glorified through all creation.

The entire Bible looks forward to a colossal time of God, to which all the struggle, need, and suffering of the present time are as nothing. But as I often have said, what is completely new and unbiblical is the idea, "It will soon be all over with me; I will shortly be dead!" No prophet or apostle ever thought that way; rather, they dwelt upon the idea, "Until our God comes! Until there comes that great time for us!" ...

If one has lived a worldly, earthbound life, the dear Lord cannot make him happy even if he is the best of men. He is too greedy for worldly things and doesn't seek the heavenly. The time of God, which finds its center in the people of Jesus Christ and the glory which is the comfort of the whole world and all its creatures — *this* is what must be sought.

REDEMPTION FROM EVIL

A *person can make himself weak by continually looking at his sinful* nature and things he sees as wrong in himself. Often the sin has been forgiven long before; but the person hangs on to it and considers himself weak and sinful. What he should do, then, is stand up and be strong, through faith in God being certain of forgiveness. . . . In principle, sin *is* forgiven; and we must carry that reality into the world.

When I *look at the conversions of today*, I *see so much lacking* that I am afraid they will be a detriment unless people stop making the conversion experience the main thing. The Lord will give nothing, will reveal nothing of that for which we hope, unless *the change of heart* remains the first and last thing. The gospel always produces repentance. . . . The outcome of one's own repentance is to produce further repentance — which thought also belongs to the gospel. But whatever does not come out of one's own repentance is about as effective as soap bubbles against fortress walls. (Johann Christoph Blumhardt)

When *people come to me in their misery*, I *always have the feeling*, "Oh, here it should be easy to help!" Even when I see a ruined body before me, or someone in the clutches of hell, I often get the powerful impression, "If only these folks had the love of God, they would be helped; but oh, the superstitions and the idols!" They think about all sorts of things, but God does not come into their hearts. . . . And so people passionately hold on to that which destroys them. This is the distress of lovelessness toward God. Don't look so much on your personal sins; nothing comes of staring at them. Hang on to God; look to him. Otherwise, even if you repent and believe, you are still not converted; your life does not depend upon God. A simple, sober reverence for God, a seeking of God in the spirit, the soul's being filled with love for God — by these we can overcome. But we must be *whole* people.

Leave for a while your begging before God and seek first the way, the way in which we truly can know God, by recognizing our guilt and in truth seeking only the righteousness of God in his rule upon earth. Put aside your own suffering and start doing honest works of repentance, doing them with joy, not with sighing and complaining, giving God the glory in body and soul. Then accept your guilt and its judgment and become a true person. Thus, through Christ, you will be bound to God; and your own suffering and need will fade of itself.

Turn about in the inward man and, instead of looking at yourself and all your need, look to the kingdom of God and its need; it has been held back for so long because of the false nature of man. Then you can be confident that God will treat you as a true child who is seeking *his* honor, and you will not come to shame in this life.

The first and last word for a disciple of Jesus is, "Obey!" I mean to say that today the word "believe" is not as important as, "You who believe, *obey* him whom you believe!" Of what use is believing if you cannot obey?

Eternal damnation is not biblical; it is only a notion of the churches. ... What the dear Lord will finally do with the disobedient is his business. *Here and now* the main thing is the battle of history; we should stick with this. What have we to do with the dear Lord's action in an entirely different age? Our concern is solely with what God wants of us in the fight that is in progress here on earth; and that, my friends, we should take seriously.

REDEMPTION FROM LAW

Our concern is not at all with the outward commandments but rather with the nature of life. That is God's commandment. Thus we find in the Bible a colossal freedom. There are none of the rules which were first formulated about the time of Jesus. Jesus goes completely beyond them; not even the law of the Sabbath is a rule for him. No sacrifice, no temple, no altar, none of them are rules for Jesus. Nothing of the outward but that of the spirit is God's law. . . .

Our people must be permeated by the simple awareness that we are God's. Accordingly, without further talk or churchly nonsense, we become both bound and free. . . . Go where you will — there is no law — *but* do it in this awareness: "I do not belong to *things*; they are no business of mine. I belong to the Father in heaven; it is with God I have to do."

REDEMPTION FROM SUFFERING

I *have for all of you a heartfelt concern before God; and I so much* want to help. However, I know of nothing to say but, "Remain firm, firm in doing what God wants." The kingdom of God must be the desire of our hearts; then solutions will come. You can be useful when you are willing to bear the greatest misery for God's sake. Even in a bodily sense you will not go under, whether or not that seems to be the case. It cannot be in vain, bearing what God wills us to bear, when we are following the one who bore the cross.

A *light-hearted Christianity is really the greatest foolishness in this* world where millions of our brothers and sisters are sinking, where everything goes dark. Therefore, the cry might well be loud, even if it comes to, "My God, my God, why hast thou forsaken me?" Correctly understood, that is not faithlessness but sympathy with the world. . . . In this cry lies our way to God and God's way to us.

The *capacity to hope is extremely important both for the kingdom* of God and for our own development, because something very real and powerful has been laid in our hearts with this hope. One might say that we have been given a power which corresponds to the power of God. A power goes forth from God to make something of us; and from us there goes forth a hope that we shall become something. And this power of God and our hope go together hand in hand, as in a marriage, walking together. We in hope and God in his power, we belong together so that we can follow a purpose, the good purpose of God.

Scarcely does a need arise and, as we think, it should be quickly cared for, because we believe in God. Yet, in this we often are disappointed. ... Frequently God goes his way high above the needs and suffering of the human way. We think that God should come with his help just as soon as is possible; but God regularly says to us, "Have patience! The goal can be reached in only one way, a way that does not permit me to suit your preference, even in giving you something very special." ... But we should not let our faith get away from us just because something was not quickly improved or made more godly. The kingdom of God entails a long, long history. All that is of God must have its own time.

CONTINUING REDEMPTION

Every disciple of Jesus can acquire some qualities of a redeemer in himself. These are gifts which God wants to give through the Holy Spirit. They then can be shared: one person has a gift for one sort of situation, another for another; but we disciples of Jesus should always have something redeeming for other people.

THE HOLY SPIRIT AND HIS GIFTS

The Holy Spirit is the Spirit of Truth. Consequently, he preaches to us in our hearts — especially in reminding us of what Jesus said, renewing this in our minds and making it ever clearer to us. And so the believing disciple carries, or ought to carry, this master teacher within himself.

Thus, it is not particularly necessary for him time and again to hear some human preacher who tells him every detail and splits hairs in explaining things. It ought not to be the case that a person is without further instruction just because no bodily teacher is present. No, the instruction continues — and just that much more powerfully because it comes not simply to the outward ears but from within, awakening the mind and spirit. Everything becomes much clearer than when one is instructed primarily through external words and still has to consider at length, "What do these words mean?"

But the Spirit, as master teacher, grants us inward revelation; we "see" what otherwise is only heard and thought. We understand profoundly, even when, now and then, words fail. Thus should the Holy Spirit be our teacher.

(Johann Christoph Blumhardt)

Our basic prayer always should be for the coming of the Holy Spirit. Of course, this is a tremendous request in itself; and it will cost us pains to put into a few words all that this petition signifies. As a very minimum, I would say, there lies in this prayer a desire to stand inwardly right before God and to come into true community with him. This is something which is mediated and accomplished by God through the Spirit. . . .

Further, our basic prayer must be that we learn to understand what is revealed to us. No one can even call Jesus Lord except through the Holy Spirit; so, to a certain extent, this idea also is expressed in our basic prayer, that God might give us an understanding of spiritual things, might let us understand his ways, his ideas about us, his plans for us. . . .

All we have said thus far represents only the preliminary stages of our prayer, for in the phrase, "Pray for the Holy Spirit," much more is being asked. At the time Jesus commanded this prayer, the disciples had not yet had the experience of Pentecost; and in that coming of the Spirit lay the salvation of all.

The one thing with which the disciples were to concern themselves was prayer for the coming of that Spirit — for themselves, for the world, for all flesh. After the Lord departed from them, that was to be their one task. We know that they did pray. Daily they were united together, praying for the promised Spirit. Together with their praying, they worked until the time was fulfilled. And on the feast of Pentecost the glorious gift and grace and power came; and they were all wonderfully filled. From that moment they truly became new men. The heavens opened, and the Lord brought the disciples into a unity with the things of heaven. Powers from above descended and covered everything upon earth. And through these powers, everything shall henceforth be overcome, and the powers of darkness shall be trampled underfoot. (Johann Christoph Blumhardt)

How is it that everything came to life wherever the apostles preached? They were not great men; they had no earthly wisdom and cleverness, no special way of speaking or gift of oratory. No, it was simply the glory of God, which, in Greece and Rome, in Macedonia and Asia Minor, in Palestine and everywhere, was bearing fruit to his honor.

[As with Paul in 2 Corinthians 12], it is quite natural that the extraordinary should come forth in a person who is truly freed and born again as a new creature, standing, therefore, in a new, totally different relationship to God from that of most people. If something striking did not show itself, we would have to doubt whether a new creature actually was present.

Now we must generalize this thought and say that, if in a Christian community nothing of the extraordinary is experienced — that is, nothing extraordinary in a recognition and experience of God, as also in a recognition and experience of the opposite, of sin and its power — then that community is in fact incapacitated.

THE LIVING CHRIST

It is an extraordinary thing and characteristic of the Lord Jesus that he gives us to understand that what he is doing on earth is only a beginning. Nothing is finished yet. Nothing is so complete, nothing so perfect, that it is to remain unchanged from what it was in his time. What he has given us is a root and not yet a tree. The seed still must grow, the branches spread out; the blossoms will come later. In the end the fruit will come. . . .

No other man ever thought, or even thinks today, that his work goes on after him in such a way that he himself is the one who continues to do it. Only Jesus has been raised above death and thus made a beginning in overcoming the death of mankind, in that he says, "As I have been, so I remain; and I *am coming*."

In this lies the nature of the cause he founded and which he represents; he represents the redemption of the race —and how can that be completed in a day? How can that be finished even in one earthly lifetime? If he had wanted only to found a party or bring to people a new variety of religion in which they could be prouder and more fanatical than in earlier ones, then he could have completed it, as Mohammed and Confucius did in their lifetimes. But, my friends, *redemption* — that requires time. It is not just for a couple of people or for a few hundred or for a party; it is for all mankind.

The Lord Jesus is the beginning and the end regarding the kingdom of God. Therefore, among us, it firmly and with certainty is said, "The Savior is coming again!" He must complete the work; and we have only to be his servants until he comes again. As servants, we must serve him, the Coming One.

At the same time, we should be a prefiguring of the future of Jesus Christ on earth. We should not be so much concerned with ourselves; nor should we struggle so hard, as though we were the ones to bring the good to its perfection on earth. We cannot do that. That can be done only by the Lord Jesus, who has come the first time and is coming again a second time.

He will complete the work; we will not. We must lock this knowledge in our hearts; it must be true and firm whenever we preach the gospel. Our way must always be lighted by this star, "He is coming again!" And if our minds are directed toward the coming of the Savior, this puts the entire gospel into its true perspective. The gospel will become something personal and living when we firmly and faithfully focus upon the words, "He is indeed coming again!" When we fail to do that, then we are separating the gospel from his person. Then, no matter how much we talk or what great speeches we make about it, we are nevertheless separating him from the gospel. Without his personal presence, not a word of the gospel has real or profound value.

And so we must be directed toward that future coming of Jesus Christ which is not only something of the future but also of the present, in that he right now is awaited in our hearts. . . .

We are living in a time of death; and we don't want to hide that from ourselves. Our powers become weak; our ideas lose their strength, and our feelings do also. Even though they be alive for the moment, with time they are lost. The law of death surrounds everything, all we do and think and feel. But now a law of life comes into this world of death. It is actually the Lord Jesus himself, the one who is eternal life, who is arisen from the dead, who links us to the other world, who brings us the Spirit of God that, in the midst of our dying life, again and again we might receive something fresh and living through his gift, through his presence, through his coming.

We are not to think of his coming only as an appearance at the end of days. Rather, we must at all times have an awareness of the coming Savior. Each of us should continually have that in mind, even in times of darkness, in times of depression, in times of poverty, in times of sickness, in times of trouble, and in times of work with the things of earth.

 We want the life of Jesus Christ to be seen completely pure and clean, to be seen alone ruling upon earth. We don't want it to be mixed with earthly arts and the things of earth; we want it to be pure Christ.

Yet this is why Christ is so hidden. He will not be on earth as a human power. Christ will not be mixed in among men as a great man among the great. What we call great is not great to God. Those things which outwardly make such an impression, which seem so heroic, which so impress us in an earthly sense — those don't impress God at all. And that is why we must take care that *we* do not become mixed.

As Christ shows himself completely pure, as he alone stands before us as the Spirit of Life, so should we Christians also remain pure and clean, not mixing ourselves with the things of our time. Every age brings forward earthly interests, and each century has its particular character. One can become part of that and also lead a satisfactory life in it; but such is not the life of God which Christ is building upon earth. That is something entirely new, which will finally conquer all that is earthly and lead to the coming of a new heaven and a new earth.

And so the life we have today must still be one of fighting and struggling for the divine. But it is a life which has great promise in it. What is hidden at present, hidden with Christ in God, finally shall be revealed. Christ, the life-bearer, the truth-bearer, who has been hidden in God for thousands of years, finally shall become clear to all eyes.

THE COMING OF CHRIST

"Behold, I am coming soon!" (Rev. 22:7). This word concerns the coming of our Lord and King, Jesus Christ. The word itself permeates the whole of his earthly and super-earthly life, and it may seem too high for our understanding to reach. There are few who can grasp it in its spiritual meaning so that it can play a natural part in their self-understanding and in their living for God. Yet we must recognize that the significance of the life of Jesus and his disciples depends upon the fulfillment of these words. Those people built upon them as a firm ground by which the results of their activity would be guaranteed. But also, all the later disciples of Jesus who carry in their hearts the kingdom of God on earth as the goal of the Christian community are directed by these words to hope for the future return of their Lord. Without that, it is useless to hope that the community of God, his justice and truth, will come upon earth.

"Behold, I am coming soon!" This saying divides the history of the Christian community into two periods: first, the foretime, and then, the time of the actual kingdom of God. The Savior himself is the beginning, the Alpha, and the end, the Omega. With the coming of the Savior in the flesh, the foretime has begun; all people should know this, for they are living in it. In this time we have the gospel, "the power of God for salvation to everyone who has faith" (Rom. 1:16). With this, the kingdom of God is announced; and through its prophets it is founded upon earth.

However, the reign of God in Christ has not yet fully penetrated our world. It has made only a quiet beginning in those who believe, and is yet unknown to the world. The faithful are but few. All the rest of mankind, the masses, even though they hear the gospel, are still under the reign of sin and death, because they are not yet able and willing to break loose from it.

Yet the light of hope does shine among these masses through the gospel, which reveals the love of God to the world. This hope is itself a world-shaking power of God which we experience in Christianity in a general way; even the unbelievers take part in that hope although they are not aware of it. It is by this power of hope coming through the gospel that the triumph of darkness is prevented; it no longer makes any headway. Wherever the gospel comes, death is pierced through by the hope of life. Yet the hearts of men are not free for God nor have they power for the victory over sin; thus, things in the world seem to go just as they always have gone.

The new (a new creation) is found only in secret, among the believers. These we can call the *forerunners* of the kingdom of God, in whom God's righteousness already has a beginning. It is their calling to be faithful unto death, to fight for the earth as being the property of God until the Son of Man comes in the glory of his Father. It is only then that the power of God in Jesus Christ will come to the peoples and to all the masses of mankind. Then will become possible that of which Christianity and the gospel are incapable in these times, namely, a judgment.

"Judgment" means that, through the rigorous Spirit of God, a person comes to know himself for who he is, making a division between what is good and what is evil in God's sight, and giving the evil over to be judged. Without such judgment, no one, even in New Testament times, was great or blessed. In the same way, it is not possible for the masses of mankind to be saved in the end without the judgment which the Son of Man brings with him when he comes. It is only in this final judgment that many things will collapse which we take as good and proper today but which in fact have been only temporarily tolerated by God.

So, regarding the world and the victory over it, all the apostles hoped for the time of Jesus' coming. Before this time, they expected no true renewal of the world as a whole. Likewise, we ought not lose faith when, for the present, the world remains untouched and our faith can fight only in secret. The world is not by that token lost forever. It awaits the final revelation of Jesus Christ in which he will show himself as King of Kings.

Of course, a lazy waiting certainly is not appropriate, for the life of the faithful is itself the beginning of the end, and upon the faithfulness of these forerunners everything depends. The Savior himself, as well as the apostles, made note of this. To those servants "who *wait* for the Lord" (Luke 12:36), "the elect who cry to him day and night" (Luke 18:7 – 8), presently there is given, as answer to their longing, the words, "Behold, I am coming soon!" Their faithfulness is a power that can bear witness to people today. Without that, the gospel does not in itself have the piercing light that makes people right and enlists them as comrades in arms in the company of Jesus Christ.

So it is a joyful thing for us to carry in ourselves the power of the gospel; it brings light into the darkness of our world and is a help toward the end-time coming of our Lord Jesus Christ, when all flesh will see the glory of God.

Time itself is our enemy. Time is the enemy of eternity. Time crinkles us up like an old towel and throws us out into the darkness of death to be forgotten, as we ourselves suffer the shame of death. Yes, time is our enemy; it brings us nothing. Christ is the one who brings something; only that which, through Christ, shall be born in the people of Christ, that is what brings the true fruit which mankind has owed to God for many, many centuries.

All the "prophecies" and booklets about the return of Christ are misleading when they suggest that the day comes according to some calculation of time. No, the day comes in response to the people of God; and changes for the good will come in response to that good which is fought for by God's people. If that does not prove a possibility, then there will come God's terrible ban against the earth (Mal. 4:1). Then a catastrophe could happen such as happened once before, with the earth again left as desolate and empty as it was before creation.

Yet, in the meantime, we must hold fast to the fact that necessary changes are not only possible but that their actuality is our one concern. The Savior has himself joined with our earth; and the Savior cannot simply be put off. . . . We can do something and should do something. We should not rest day or night. "Things must be *different!*" — that should be the continuous cry of our hearts.

And what can we do? We can take the guilt upon ourselves.

There are parties in Christendom who are already rejoicing that they will be transfigured and float up to heaven and then will laugh at the poor people left behind. But that is not the way it is. Now is the time to take upon ourselves a work in which *we* are the first to be given into judgment, not the first to have a sofa in heaven. For only those who are truly first, first to stand before the Savior in judgment, can become tools to further his work among the rest of mankind.

"And this is the name by which he will be called: 'The Lord is our righteousness' " (Jer. 23:6). Such texts are very important to me, because they are concerned with the last times, the times which we usually think of in terms of the dark king, the desolation, Antichrist. Admittedly, it is written that there are enemies and opposition, as also an Antichrist. Yet scripture does not speak of any all-powerful Antichrist.

On the other hand, over and over again scripture does tell of a King who will bring peace over all the earth, thus making the end a culmination of the *good*. Oh, yes, people speak of the culmination of *evil*. Now, indeed, that *is* our experience. But scripture speaks of the end as the culmination of good; it is not the good but evil that shall be overthrown. Even before he comes, the Lord will be master of the earth. For, when he comes, we must then be able to say, "The Lord is our righteousness!"

(Johann Christoph Blumhardt)

THE SPIRIT WORLD

It is not the case that we are little manikins and there is the great, tremendous, powerful God of whom it is difficult for us to think, let alone understand. Rather, the reign of God operates through an endless number of powers, through an endless number of the heavenly host, through an endless number of personalities that stand about his throne and stand near to us as well.

Yes, I know quite well that modern man wants to see only people and, beyond them, nothing else in the whole, wide world. I know very well that we want to be the only ones who have the Spirit, thus glorifying ourselves. . . . But, my friends, everything which lives in the heavenly world — that world into which our material eyes cannot see, which fills all earth and heaven — those beings nevertheless surround us from the side of the Father in heaven. There exists a regime under which we repeatedly feel ourselves served by invisible powers; and time and again our spirit feels awakened by the Spirit which fills the whole creation and which is God.

I don't want to have a single day go by without recalling that God's heavenly host is around us, going out into all the world. I couldn't live a single day without the thought that there is never a time nor a place that we are alone.

God sends us all sorts of powers, all sorts of helpers, both corporeal and spiritual; and all these messengers of God are personal in nature. Under God's command, there are an endless number of powers which can surround us and accompany us; and they are most various.

For a long time we have fought against darkness. The devil, death, and hell would have us in terror. We have been in many difficulties, and many times have not seen a way through. But God has reached out his right hand to us in Jesus Christ; and for many years he has protected us and given us victory. But today there appears another fight for us, namely, the fight against people who do not want to accept the truth. Yet more dangerous than the invisible powers of darkness is the visible power of men, those who falsely administer the power of God, who misuse the Spirit in their flesh and so put God's honor to shame through their cunning. More dangerous than the deceptions of the world are deceptions in the name of Christianity.

We experience many things which are not at all meant to be shared with others. Regarding experiences connected with the kingdom of God, it is not the main thing that others know about them — except, perhaps, that others might live on the fruit of an individual's experience of the kingdom. But the private experiences of Jesus and the apostles, as those of the prophets of the Old Testament, are for the most part untold.

We are convinced and could adduce much scripture showing that an unfathomable knowledge of the invisible world — the human-demonic-satanic as well as the divine — formed the background for the theory of the apostles and prophets, if I may put it so. Yet they do not favor us with glimpses of their experiences in this realm. Their thought runs, "If a person is called to participate in the battle, it is hardly necessary for us to tell him how it is. He will see for himself just how things are there where the earthly eyes of men do not penetrate." . . .

It is not the devil to whom we want to give importance but our beloved God; and it is people, not demons, who should now put in an appearance. . . .

Even the fighters themselves keep their distance from associations within this battle in which they are engaged. . . . It is not their task to give visible people a story of the invisible world. . . . Their call, indeed, is to prove themselves God's true fighters to whom nothing counts except the kingdom of God in *this* world.

There are not two worlds, one in God's hand and the other not. There are not two varieties of humans, one within God's rule and the other outside. No, even where it is utterly dark, God alone is Lord. There is no devil who can do whatever he wills, no evil angel who can create anything; the fact that these are *in the darkness* is itself "of God." Unfortunately, there is in the darkness a certain form of life which spreads and brings death to those who allow themselves to be drawn into it. Yet, despite the sway of sinful and death-dealing powers, that whole realm belongs to God and remains firmly in his hand. This is the witness we can have in our hearts. To every satan I would like to say, "You are God's, you satan. You can do nothing; you can't lift a finger, for you are God's."

We have never yet believed in the devil. That is why, fifty-five years ago, we said, "Jesus is victor." He alone is victor; there is no lord, even in the darkness, who does not have to bow to *our* Lord. There is but *one* Lord, just as there is but *one* God; and nothing else is lord. Nothing else has any power. Nothing else has any rights or can claim anything as its own; no hell or death or devil can claim as much as a nail. Everything belongs to our God — yes, *everything*. If we would take such a position, then the darkness would have to go. . . . Fear no thing; fear God alone.

FANATICISM AND IRRATIONALITY
(An Afterthought)

It is fanaticism when a person regularly thinks only in natural terms, believing that he receives help only through the natural order. *That* is irrational. Yet even to the present day, a person is called irrational and heretical if he has hope in the Holy Spirit and the power of God.

One thing is certain. Biblically, that which is only "of the world" is irrational; and it is fanaticism when one abandons oneself to such stuff as, in the world, regularly is offered as aid and comfort. If I did not have to be discreet, I could gather a bouquet composed of letters from those who believe themselves to be rational in comparison to others. Yet we could see into what colossal irrationalism worldly people enter — and little wonder, with their wanting nothing from God, or at least nothing directly from him. Nevertheless, those whom *they* call fanatic and treat as irrational, those are the ones who stay rational by resting their hope upon the testimonies of God.

MANKIND

GOD AND MAN — HUMANITY'S BECOMING HUMAN

It has always been my experience that whoever is an enemy of men is also an enemy of God. Whoever will not recognize the good that is in man, God will not recognize either. Whoever judges men, whoever damns men, whoever wants nothing to do with the people he sees as being "the least" — that person is himself separated from God. May things happen to him as they will.

We would become Men. Men, not "Christians" — Men! Not Catholics, not Protestants — Men! Not Conservatives, not Liberals, not Socialists — Men! Not French, not German, not Chinese — "Men"! It was as a man Jesus became the light of the world; and it is men he would have.

*True man is missing.... False men with a false spirit, with false desires and false aims, think that they are real men. ... The false man is the world's undoing. ... True man is still missing and will be missing until Jesus comes and does away with the false man....

Yet now we do have the fortune to know that there is one in whom the world is God's again, in whom all that is created is

---

*At this point, Ragaz used an excerpt from a sermon that appears in its entirety in Lejeune's *Christoph Blumhardt and His Message* (pp. 157– 68). I have chosen to replace Ragaz's selection with a somewhat broader one of my own, using the Plough Publishing House translation, although taking the liberty to change the order of some of Blumhardt's sentences in the interest of a smoother reading. — V. E.

again placed into the light of the first creation. This one is Jesus. ... Jesus, the Son of Man, is more real than any other man, more childlike than all other children. He lives among men, and he is the kingdom of God. He does not *make* it; he *is* the kingdom! Why? Because he is God and man.

When God created the world he founded his kingdom on earth. The earth was his kingdom. And who was to reign, to rule, and to watch over it as his representative? Man. God's kingdom was in paradise through man. God's kingdom is on earth through one upright man, no matter what men are like otherwise.... One true man — and God's kingdom is here! ... An Adam, and there it was, God himself in paradise. Even if here and there something wrong was still lurking in corners, that didn't matter. A man was there, and God was with this man. Nothing else was of any importance....

The loss of man was the world's catastrophe. Man was gone. This is still the world's undoing today. ...

Now Jesus seeks a *living church*, and he seeks it on earth. Could not the one who rose from the dead have come quickly, in heavenly glory, to conquer and overcome all things? He would have done it long ago, without hesitating, if this would have made God's kingdom possible. He could have come with hosts of angels. But no! He doesn't want only angels. Man, not superworldly powers, must serve God on earth. True man must do it; and God must do it in him. This is Jesus' loyalty toward us false men.

OF THE GREATNESS, FREEDOM, AND GLORY OF MAN

Now earth has not only its life but also its consciousness — and this last is Man. The earth's faculty of consciousness is man. In spite of all the sunshine and moonlight, the splendor of the stars and the greenness of grass and forest — in spite of all, it is a dark matter if earth, in its conscious mind, does not know the truth, which is to say, if the Son of God is not recognized. Man must recognize him in order that, by him, the consciousness of the earth might reach fulfillment.

Because everything we ask for [in the opening petitions of the Lord's Prayer] ultimately involves our own benefit, God does not make it his business to see that his name is kept hallowed, that his kingdom come, that his will be done — unless these things are, at the same time, the request of man. God will not make it his business if we do not find it important enough to hold his name in honor throughout the world; to oppose all that is willed contrary to the will of God; to help gather all creatures into the kingdom in order that his mastery of the earth might be attained. Consequently, God lets things happen as they will and as men want them to.

Even so, there are countless people who do not ask after the name of God nor trouble themselves at all concerning him. Again, some people would prefer anything other than being gathered into a kingdom of God. And how many there are who know absolutely only their own wills or who let themselves be led only by the will of darkness. But God will not use force and compel his creatures into their salvation. They shall, then, have that which they bring upon themselves, shall have all that great misery which people fall into who are without God, separated from God, or opposed to God.   (Johann Christoph Blumhardt)

The work of the kingdom of God must stand under two laws. First, you dare never again be angry at anyone, for the kingdom of God is love for all men. Therefore, you may not belittle anyone, even the least. Indeed, you are a miserable fool if you vex or annoy one of these little ones, demean him, or treat him as nothing. Thus, we must always look with God's evaluation upon what I like to call "the pennies of God's capital investment." They belong to God, of course, although the value lies in the persons themselves. As man, you are of value to God; yet, your value is not a hair greater than that of some little guy of no status, e.g., a day-laborer. We always must bear in mind the worth

God attributes to a small, low-ranked, despised human being; such people we must guard and protect.

The second law is that we remain *slaves*. Slaves we want to be; lords we want never to become. We would be slaves under God's hand — yet, that I not be misunderstood: slaves of men we will never be! ... If I serve God, then God will stand by me and men must give way to me. I shall not yield as much as a fingernail to any man. And if empires and kingdoms of men multiply until the very heavens and earth itself fall, yet shall I stand like a rock in the sea. I hold fast to God, I am *his* slave; and all must break itself to pieces upon me, because I serve God.

We *should be priests, i.e., we who have become firm in grace* should stand firm for others, praying for them and the world so that the whole might be filled with the glory and power and grace of God. If we are steadfast in this priestly sense, then we bear a *kingly* power. We can cooperate in overcoming the dark powers of this world. ... You are not to be priests for yourselves but for the world in which you live. That world should move your heart; and if you see something of its misery and death, then you should protest against it, saying, "That cannot be; indeed, it must cease, because Jesus lives."

NO NONENTITIES

Whoever is demeaned and troubled has the sympathy of God. I might even say that our dear God can't see our *sins* for the sheer *suffering* that is present, his heart welling up in love for the lowly ones in this world upon whom people wrongly pass judgment. ... All sufferers, through their very suffering, should become bound to God. ... The sufferer should be so positioned that he comes to experience great *friendship*, while the suffering itself comes to be identified as the *enemy* of both God and man, interposing itself between them. The suffering, then, becomes a third party, the one that is to be evicted from the house.

The Savior has two sides which make him great. The one side is that he recognizes people as his own, seeing in them his own property. Also, he can communicate with them, instantly establishing a relationship with whomever he will.

But he also has a second side by which people understand him and can easily develop a relationship *from themselves to him*. One thing cannot be denied: there is no individual so outwardly and so inwardly degenerate that, when he encounters the Savior, does not feel, "He truly wants *me!*" Immediately that person comes alive and, at the same time, discovers Jesus in his heart. Then there comes a sense of community — and after that, *no questions are asked. . . .* Jesus never demands character references. Such is the *human* way: scoundrels here, scoundrels there! But the force of the good in Jesus brings out the goodness in people, entirely overlooking the evil, which is spoken of no more. . . . Let us, also, not so much look upon the old man as help the new one come forth.

NO ONE BAD OR GODLESS

The worst is when we Christians want to make people different. Where has our dear God said that we should convert people? Nowhere is that said. . . . People cannot make themselves better simply because we wish it. Conversion does not happen according to our will, but according to God's.

My friends, you must never look upon people as being weeds, or tares. The tares which are harvested as the sheaves (Matt. 13:24–30) — those are not people themselves. We would make a great error if we were to say, "*These* men are tares, and *those* are wheat." No; oh, no! Consider that what we see as evil, as criminal, as sinful in people — of all these things *we also* bear the trace, even though we already venture to call ourselves children of God, body and soul. Who presumes to look into the depths of human nature? There, we are all alike.

Yet, on the surface, in the outer sphere of life, the law-breaking that shows up often is directed against human laws, not divine ones. There, pushing up, is the vile, criminal nature which is the outgrowth of the tares, crowding out the wheat kernels and stalks so that even a truly noble person becomes an evildoer.

I venture to assert, indeed, I dare say it before God: we must guard ourselves from making this malicious distinction. Strike out against evil we must — but, for God's sake, don't damn *people*! These old tares that have been scattered throughout Christendom — for God's sake, don't see them as being people! We poor people, we are all tangled up in them.

Have you ever seen the wind in a grainfield? There is little one can do to stop it; it tears up the delicate plants and destroys them. And so it goes with many people. Somehow a seed has come into their neighborhood and now is growing in an inhuman and unnatural way. It grows all through people, pushing into their feelings, influencing their wills. Often we label them as fools because of their behavior; and, consequently, they are put down and considered by us as "sinners." Yet, if we were to think about it, the trace of those scattered seeds could be found even in our own lives.

Therefore, in all we are called to do in the way of holding human society together, the greatest blessing is this: although humanly we have to distinguish between righteousness and unrighteousness, these distinctions go no further than our own opinion. Would you go so far as to damn people for eternity? Do you want to take over the work of God? Is it then, O man, that *you* would make eternal decrees?

LOVE AND COMMUNITY

We must have a sense of community. Individual development, indeed, is also useful, particularly as a grounding for Christianity; yet, we still need this sense of community. And it should be built upon the truth that belongs to it, namely, the law of God. . . .

You should keep the law of God. You should learn what you are to do by listening to the person of Christ; and you will need no other teacher. Only in this way is community possible. If a person exists only for himself, he will have a very hard time of it and scarcely succeed.

Don't believe it — that a person can become blessed and happy by himself. You, on earth, have been called into the community of Jesus Christ; we depend upon each other — and when one member suffers, the others suffer also. We must *perceive* one another in the Holy Spirit so that we can *serve* one another even as we let ourselves be served. Just as, out of this sense of community, God asks you to serve others as often as you have opportunity, just so, at another point, he asks you to let yourself *be served* — even by a person you may consider beneath you — that thereby you might know that *you* are nothing and God is everything and might learn to regard the other person as higher than yourself. . . .

Above all, the *fruit* of this community with God and with one another must be that all sin is covered. . . . Indeed, this quality of community exists precisely that sin might be overcome. . . . Consequently, our sin must there be hidden; and we must always be ready to testify as to where that sin has been placed.

Many times a person can push through to faith by himself. . . . But in difficult cases, a person cannot do this on his own. Consider, my friends, I am nothing in myself; I am what I am only through this sort of community. If there are no brothers and sisters who understand me, I am nothing. . . . In the kingdom of God, no one exists for himself. We exist through God's grace — and to do that is to exist *for* others and *with* others and to have ever more of the sense of community so that we can become a single instrument of power.

All the bonds of secular society, whether among heathen or Christians, represent *imprisonment* insofar as men are bound to men. In this way, a person becomes entangled with other people, finally achieving a human sort of union in which one individual pulls against another at his pleasure. And sad to say, that which generally is called "the church" has not kept free or been spared from this danger.

What comes under the generic term "church" and constitutes so-called "Christendom" has become simply a collection of sects and parties. And in that setup, one always has a bad conscience before others or is embarrassed before them; one goes "the way of men" along with the others to whom he has bound himself. Consequently, anxiety is created; there is a strong group spirit which must be respected. And so a person has to bow and scrape himself off the street and into the church. All in all, it is a very unpleasant story. And thus, frequently, it is seen that this sort of curse does not hold the person for long before he returns to entirely secular society.

But, dear friends, you are created after the image *of God* and not according to human images. There is no human image to which you must conform. There is only God the Father, whose likeness you can adopt. It is something impossible that you, in the long run, can endure by means of the human and transient or by making yourself dependent upon the endurance of the human. Rather, you should take note that you then do irreparable damage to your soul; and who is going to fix that for you?

Yet, my friends, it is the case that we have a *new* covenant, a covenant in which we all take on the image of God. It is not a bond in which we make this or that law and try to differentiate ourselves from other people. There is no looking down on others. Other people have no authority over you, and you have no authority over others. There is only one bond — one true covenant in Christ. There is no law putting people over people. In Christ, there is only the law of God, from the Father in heaven. And when this law stands fast in every heart, there is a loving, free, blessed sense of community among us.

Then the manipulating, hurting, repulsing judgment will entirely cease in our midst. Then, in this love toward God, we shall, one with another, be impassioned toward *one* object and do our loving one with another. And we shall do this even

55

though one person or another has different opinions, a different creed, or understands things differently (perhaps even better) than we do. Then there will be no more of the human bonding from which comes war and bloodshed. Then there will be the bonding of God which, in all our hearts, the Holy Spirit will be able to certify as nothing but love, nothing but the sense of true community.

The question today, as at the time Jesus appeared, is whether we can arrive at such a relationship and such a covenant.

What we usually call "love" is something that makes us weak. Therefore, among people in general, it is at the urging of their nature that they hate their enemies. Only a person who is born of God can do what Jesus says. Of course, if we are motivated from below, if we are mastered by our passions — sympathies and antipathies — then we cannot truly love. One must, therefore, be a child of God. And how does one become that? . . . We are such by nature. . . . We are from God. Consequently, something of his Spirit should live in us, should pluck us out of the ordinary to lift and carry us.

The love which friends or lovers have toward one another does not accomplish anything toward loving the *enemy!* The person who offends me, who does not understand me, who regularly humiliates and scolds me — he's the one to hold fast for God: "You belong to me because you have hurt me." If we always cut ourselves off and separate ourselves from those who do not please us, is the goal then reached? For that matter, what *is* our goal? . . . Is is not that God's love should once master the whole world and that all the brutal acts and the suffering caused by those acts forever disappear? Then, if we take part in this by being patient and loving, isn't that worthwhile? . . . We are drawing into the world the power which yet shall win the victory.

I know of no greater light coming from Jesus than this: "Love your enemies." That is the word which should get its turn today.

The individual heart is very like a police headquarters; there people's deeds are arranged as in a file drawer. One has only to ask, "What do you have on that person? What have you on this one?" The person can open the file and give out information on anyone. . . . Very often, with real grace, we leave the drawer closed and do not talk about the cases; yet, when necessary, the key is still there so that the cases can be brought to light. And that hinders; it does harm.

As long as we have a police register in our hearts, it is impossible for us to do anything with others. With this file drawer in my heart, even if I say something of great significance to someone, it still won't do. The clear speaking of the will of God becomes possible only after the file drawer has been destroyed. We must be as firm as a rock in this matter: I will not be a police headquarters; the cases shall no longer be entered in *me*! Once take that stand and you will see how the illumination of your heart increases and how light its troubles become. Even the evil world loses its heaviness and everything goes well because the light of the Savior's life now can illumine us.

Jesus will *bear the guilt*; but he will *not* be present in a heart in which there is a police station. He does not go in; he does nothing there. He *has borne* the guilt of the world; and if you are one who *lays on* guilt, he may not have anything to do with you. That being so, take thought!

Give a person this consciousness: "I am God's" —and immediately he will climb out of all his misery. The first thing that happens when a person is lost is that he sinks under. Thus our love should be such that we communicate this consciousness both to ourselves and to others. We should not put down either ourselves or others, should not consider anyone as evil.

Our love should be like the sunshine, as Jesus himself said. It should shine upon everyone and itself remain light and clean. In this way, our power would remain powerful. The enemy would be able to sense that we are not out to correct him but to accept him as God's child. Then he would no longer be an enemy. But when the world becomes insulting about this or that and we join in, then we have lost the consciousness that we are God's.

Jesus sees every person as abnormal but gives up no one as lost. If people were not as they are, they would have no need of salvation. So, in the next place, Jesus allows all to come to him *as they are*: sinners and righteous, poor and rich, healthy and sick. Jesus gives himself to each person as he is; and people ought not play up their own piety and put down that of others.

Jesus wishes only that his disciples *serve*, as he himself served in the very shedding of his blood. His disciples, in his spirit, should make others free, giving up on nobody but, in great forbearance, looking for the good that God has created in each one. Once a person is thus freed, he can readily correct himself. This is how it is: always directed by a spirit of serving, saving, and freeing, we can fight against the greatest powers, certain of victory even in the most difficult relationships.

GODLY HUMANNESS

If we observe the life of the Savior and ask, "Which way did he go regarding people?" we find that he always sought out the childlike, the simple, the unsophisticated. But whatever was nailed into place, whatever attempted to be "religious" in a legalistic sense — from all of that he kept his distance.

Therefore, today I say: The ways which consist so much in "outwardness," with their outward laws and outward activities . . . the ways upon which there is to be seen only the earthly life fenced in on religious grounds and the people weighed down with burdens . . . these are broad ways upon which anyone can go. And yet — and always on the grounds of "the religious life" — a person will increasingly be seen frequenting these ways as his "inwardness" becomes stunted, as the true power of his spirit dies away and, with it, the power of the eternal God as well.

It is not good that Christendom has been established solely

by law. Indeed, if into this purely legal Christendom there also had not regularly come childlike individuals, often directly out of the masses, out of uneducated circles, out of the circles of the scorned and lowly ... if such childlike individuals had not found a way of saying, "I'm getting away from all this; I'm a child of God; and if I am being despised, then all people are being despised" ... if it had not been for these people, the Christian community would not have done as well as it has.

But this is terrible, my friends; everywhere among men you find wisdom, learning, might, rule, influence, every possible disposition. But only at great cost can you find childlikeness, the childlike heart. Under all the confusion of teaching and learning, under all the cultured manners, very often true man lies dead. What society most often makes of us is *slaves*! Many are not capable of thinking through what "the people" are saying; and so they look around and wind up going the way that all "the people" are going.

Have you not noticed that childlike individuals most often are looked upon by others as evil? I can think of many who were looked at cross-eyed their entire lives, simply because of their childlike demeanor, even though there was truth and the power of living in them. Many such people never get recognized, because childlikeness is of no use to our society. It needs clever and ruthless people who can exercise power over others; but the childlike must always seem to be on its way out. As the Lord Jesus, in his childlikeness and humility, had to stand against the religious laws of his day and thus get himself murdered, so it still goes today.

A *person must be converted twice; once from the natural man to* the spiritual, and then again from the spiritual man to the natural.
(Johann Christoph Blumhardt)

THE NEW REVELATION

I *am truly pleased by the question,* "Does what once was said long ago to the people of that time apply also to *us*?" Indeed, this was also the question of my life, the answer coming to me only with difficulty. The question was solved not only theoretically but practically, being set forth through an act of God so that then we could say, "Now it applies to us; and even if it did not fully happen with the biblical people, it can now happen with me." Thus something is happening for us today which did not take place for Abraham or Moses or even one of the apostles.

The advance of the kingdom of God brings to light old *and new* demands, as these may be required, and also old *and new* promises. There is nothing rigid, nothing mechanical about the rule of our God. Everything is always new, alive, relevant, and timely. And our problem, then, is always to understand what it is that is going on *today*.

Meanwhile, I believe, we have to *seek* — on the basis of the conscientious belief that Jesus is the truth of God — to seek that which today is true to life and to the living promises of God. I can understand that you — and many people — find this doubtful. Yet the old gives way; and new necessities bring forward new graces. And until this last is firmly understood, we will continue to stagger about. In this you can trust: whoever seeks will find, because God is never lost. However, he will be found only where he is, not letting himself be found where he does not wish to be. In this way, then, we must *seek* him.

A*part from life-experiences it does not happen. We dare boldly to* say that "revelation" is also needed *today*; it did not terminate with the Bible. I am well aware that many people get angry over the word "revelation" and consequently, out of their very piety, have quarreled over all of God's direct actions and his many miraculous deeds. But I do not see why, out of small-mindedness, we should allow the Highest to be robbed of what is his.

Christ lives; and if he lives, then there also is revelation; and revelation is essential for the hearts of those who would be enlightened by God.

On this basis [i.e., a new development of the kingdom of God penetrating the world] it is now permitted us to think of all things as being new. And if, for example, the apostles earlier have said, "Whoever believes is blessed, but whoever does not believe is damned; blessedness to those who believe, woe to those who do not" — that, in the course of the centuries, has changed a bit. Today it means: "Be blessed! Be blessed also for your enemies, for your opponents — be blessed even for the unbelievers!" We must be a people of blessing for the whole world; then the kingdom of God will come in blessedness.

THE BIBLE

If *we are awaiting a new* Zion [i.e., a new Jerusalem, which is the new church community of the redeemed people of God], then, in our hearts we must prepare for *that* Zion and disregard the position presently defined by anyone's church confession. In our hearts we must make ready to serve God alone. And if we become fellow workers with God toward that end, then we will again be *biblical*. It certainly is no fine or helpful word to call a person "biblical" simply because he follows and is zealous for the confessions.

The "biblical" keeps itself *free*. Thus, as it has always been, so today it also is difficult to seek and to give expression to that which is of God. Rather, so much of the human has found expression that the "biblical" now appears as some sort of defense for our civil and social life. Thus it can happen that finally someone with a *biblical* truth must be willing to be seen as a corrupter of the state and of the church.

Yet even so, Christ the Cornerstone stands eternal; and from this Stone ever and again will come "the new" — until heaven and earth are themselves made new and the old has gone down before the new, in-streaming kingdom of God.

People speak much these days about "the inspiration of scripture"; and this is good. However, I prefer to speak of "inspired people." God be thanked that we have scriptures that came from those through whom God's Spirit spoke the truth. Yet it is the *prophet* who is inspired, not the letter of scripture. And if the letter is to lead to the truth, so must you also be led by the Spirit of God as you read.

Conversely, today's natural man knows nothing of the Spirit of God and so gets himself quite confused regarding the words of the inspired prophets. But thus, also, a man like Luther could, for *his* time, personally witness to the God-intended truth of that for which other writers of *his* time could find no meaning nor make any sense. He was ruled by God and the Spirit, not by biblical texts. But if we all attend only upon the revealed life of God, and if each person is zealous only for his own gifts regarding God's truth and steadfastness, then we do not need to be in conflict over the inspiration of scripture. We then can find ourselves in reciprocal agreement.

Even in ancient times there was a distinction: God in Yahweh (Jehovah) and God in the totality of the world. Thus the heathen stood under God, but Israel under God in Yahweh — and Yahweh is the colleague who lives *with man*. Originally the name Yahweh was a cry, "He is here!" When something happens as one of the gracious acts of God, that signifies, "He is here!" As Jacob lay with a stone for his pillow and saw the ladder to heaven, he said, "He is here!" And thus there was built up a concept of God's entirely loving actions signifying *Yahweh*. Indeed, in this regard there is nothing more grand than the Old Testament. Veritably, God lived with man; and man knew him through his deep and wonderful acts.

Consider once how poor we would be if we did not know of these gracious acts of God. If we always had to think of God in philosophic modes, how could we ever truly speak *of* him or *to* him? Yet every child can know this: God is like a father who does good to his children, who will be humane toward mankind. And because of these gracious acts of God, we are now, in particular, to be reconciled *in Christ*. It is there, indeed, that God has come in the flesh, has revealed himself as flesh. . . . Jesus would be truly human man, on that account calling himself the Son of Man; and in him, God himself draws near to man.

One must have norms, even for the Bible. And in this case it is

63

Christ, as he is presented by the apostles. Wherever in scripture I cannot make that norm fit, then that passage is not for me until I *can* make it fit. Many times, then, I must wait until the teaching comes, until finally it is given to me.

(Johann Christoph Blumhardt)

"*They will sit at thy feet and learn of thy words*" (*Deut. 33:3*, according to Blumhardt's German translation). When you place yourself before that which our beloved God has *spoken*, then you are at the feet of God. Yet this happens only when one *believes* that it does. Many people do not take this personally enough, and God withdraws; then the word remains hidden and no longer has *power*. Consequently, many no longer take it as the word of God and want nothing more to do with it. A person must watch himself that he does not take the word of God too humanly, too superficially.

That which God has spoken represents his *Person*. I would almost like to say, "Don't give me the word as though *it* were something — not the Bible but *God in the Bible*." . . . One can use the Bible in a fearful, superstitious way if one looks only on the outward aspect of what it says, sticking to the letter rather than simply accepting that *God* is present in it. Now, if I read the Law, I am also speaking with God. This way a person can understand the Bible quite simply, because he hears God speak to him. There comes to him an understanding quite different from what otherwise would be the case. But when the person fails to do this sort of reading, he is being unbiblical. He is not understanding the Bible, because he is not taking it as something *God* says. If we translate everything coming to us from God into *human* terms, then we have a system; and that means that the "biblical" and, indeed, the essential Bible itself are utterly lost. . . .

So it goes continually with everything one should say and hear: if he does it as seated at the feet of God, it will have a totally different effect from what it would if he simply read a book. Doing *that* has no real value. . . . It is not the book that has value; it is *persons* that have value — in this case, the Person of *God*.

64

Therefore, I will sit at the feet of God; *there* I will learn — today so, tomorrow so, come what may!

One must, in his Bible reading, also notice how earthly things around us are going. There one inevitably discovers that things are not as they stand in the Bible; and it is easy, then, to say, "Because we do not have it so, apparently such things are not to be." But that is a false conclusion. We should be honest enough to say, "If we do not have these things, then they should and must *come to be.*"

It is true that, in the Bible, we now have certain decrees of God by which we can judge whether someone is remaining faithful to *the* decree of God. But for the advance of the kingdom we need — pardon my expression — more than the Bible; we need *direct instruction.*

THE FALL OF CHRISTENDOM

FROM THE SPIRIT TO THE LETTER

What can we do that the life of God might be in us? What stands in the way? A current mode of biblical scholarship. These scholars have murdered the Savior with the Old Testament and are now assaulting him with the New. We must follow that which the Spirit of God speaks to our hearts — even if it is something not completely expressed in the Bible. We should be free people, free from forms and books and the dictates of men, hearing and acting according to what the Spirit of God tells us.

There is a certain Bible-spirit that takes away everything which should be heard in such a way that it remains a word for our time spoken directly by God. That spirit leaves us, instead, with the impotent letter.

THE DENIAL

Today the apostles stand as a sign and wonder in the world. A fire of the almighty God went out from them in apostolic fashion, not in words but in power.

Yet, to a real extent, this apostolic activity ended with a stroke upon the death of the apostles. . . . Obviously, the Foundation Stone no longer could be eliminated from the world; but the divine, unmediated progress of heavenly demonstrations upon earth, the immediate revelations of God among men, these were over. People helped themselves by means of *memories*; and in this way there could be truly pious people and many times, also, intimations of Zion [i.e., of the redeemed community of the new Jerusalem]. Here and there a light still flashed. But in general, that of God was overwhelmed by "the human". . . . Human cleverness came up like mushrooms. Heathenish systems got mixed into the true Christian faith. . . . War and bloodletting marked the course of Christendom.

FROM THE KINGDOM OF GOD TO "RELIGION"

You are God's. . . . You need only the self-knowledge that God can show you; you don't need "religion."

Our worlds break apart; they don't last. But God's world is established upon the *word* of God; and that is eternal. . . .

These worlds, or cultures, which man has made — whether they be Chinese or European — all collapse together. But God be praised, while they are falling, we can smile — if, through the fall of these carnal worlds, we hold firm to and assert God's law and in no way let ourselves be deflected from striving for *his* world. Such a disposition of the heart and such a striving of the spirit, these alone will lead us to where we can experience the advance of the kingdom of God.

Recently, in another country, I met a person with whom I had a passing conversation touching upon religion. He expressed this view: "There is no *progress* in religion; we have learned that much. It is always the same. In all other works of the human spirit there *is* progress. Religion alone keeps its seat." I cringed but had to say, "Yes, you are right!"

But in *the truth* there is progress. The truth imparts *life*; but no invention of the world can give us progress in life. It is in *righteousness* that progress must come; but no invention of the world makes men good and upright. Most of all, it is *the kingdom of God* that represents progress. And in God's kingdom there is none of the old "sitting on the spot"; for the kingdom of God consists in the coming of the truth and righteousness of our God.

Where would we be if we had only "religion" which was expressed in certain teachings — and these were all we had to live by and to present before our neighbors? No, the one thing that is truly alive is the hope of a new day for man. But take that hope out of its Christian context, and it no longer exists at all; it is not aroused through some religion or other.

"Having Christianity" is nothing difficult. Concerning one "Christianity" — for there are several varieties — a person can hardly avoid it; he comes into it simply by being born, and it causes him no great trouble to stay in. It might cause him a bit of trouble actually to live it out; but whoever wants to can do so blithefully.

Yet there is another sort of Christianity that is to be enclosed within the heart — this one called "the rule of God upon earth." It is to be so enclosed in the heart that one knows for a certainty, "It will come to be!" And that Christianity many times will make us anxious and sorrowful.

It seems right to me that the Lord Jesus should have said, in effect, "Children, it is on the very turf of Christianity and the following of Jesus that there will be the most lies, the most power plays of darkness trying to destroy us."

It isn't pretty but is nevertheless true that, on the spot where the Highest and Holiest is fighting for our eternity, there is taking place the most deception and error. And it is all the more dangerous that precisely there error takes on the appearance of truth, because words can play so important a role. It always has been dangerous, in the area of the religious life and the following of Jesus, that words have meant so much. Yet words don't produce anything all that important; only actions are truly creative. And unless God leads his people into action — people whose only purpose is to follow — then nothing will go forward.

We have taken pains to emphasize that we are not to identify our Christianity with Christ himself.... We have sought to explain how Christendom is, so to speak, a secondary world in which

Christ is honored as God—although only in the way the world speaks of God. Thus, as the world *speaks* of God without becoming godly, so the secondary world of Christendom speaks of Christ without following him.

A person speaks of faith *in* Christ yet produces no faith *for* Christ (to use). . . . He believes *in* the love of God which was in Christ but does nothing *for* (or in response to) the love of God. He believes *in* eternal life but does not believe in doing anything *for* (or about) eternal life. He believes *in* the kingdom of God; he does not believe anything *for* (the sake of) the kingdom of God. So faith, hope, and love are only words if the *actions* die within us; and all the noisy gongs and clanging cymbals of Christendom, this secondary world which still invokes Christ, cannot hide that wretched death.

W*ould it be too much to say that, in Christendom, Christ is dead* and Christians have returned to the sin of the ancient people of God?

Not with "strange gods" perhaps—although Christians may not be entirely free of that—but of themselves they have throttled the God-longing within themselves; and it is now the varieties of Christianity of every form that strive for the highest spot. If formerly the totality of mankind built the Tower of Babel, we now see *the Christian churches* building that tower. T*hey* want to be infallible, to be the greatest and most clever. T*hey* figure things out; and *they* will suppress God's word and, with their own words, bring in the kingdom.

[Referring to Matthew 11:25–30, Blumhardt says:] *that was* the time when the Lord Jesus felt himself forsaken but where, in the little land of Galilee, the simple people began to bring him joy. But those who were rulers among men had quickly turned away.

And that is how it always goes among us: that which the Lord Jesus would give, such people are the first not to want it. Whether they are now people of love and goodwill or, as then in Jerusalem, people of pride and arrogance, these rulers who dominate human culture are always and everywhere present.

And the greatest goodheartedness and kindness in a populace, even the best of wills, is of no advantage regarding that for which Jesus came. He came to raise mankind completely out of earthly things and into the heights of God. And in doing that, he first of all forces earthly things *out* of the heights of God. And no society is about to let that happen.

So it has been, even to the present day. One can, in a manner of speaking, *enculturate* Christianity and even bring it to power; but then it is no longer what Jesus had in mind. Even such "Christian" powers — which ultimately are in opposition to the Spirit of God — will be displaced by other powers or else become bound up with them; and the whole world will again be running on the same old tracks. There is no track driving through to Christianity.

We *dare not surrender that which we so long have carried in the* heart, namely, that, to the glory of God, the Savior might reveal himself in new ways. This is, indeed, a great offense to many people, because, in present-day Christendom, everyone thinks he can see what is needed for the fulfillment of God's will upon earth. I very much wish that I could do that, hopeful of what I might observe in the various forms of Christianity. However, I am not able to do so; for everywhere there is untruth and unrighteousness which in some way must be removed if, in *its* truth and righteousness, the kingdom of God is to become public fact.

I grant you that there are now also many people who object that the Bible gives us no warrant at all for waiting any longer — as does even a Christian "religion," in suggesting that, after death, one becomes blessed and continues so until the end of the world. Yet perhaps one may be permitted to think a bit differently regarding the scriptures. And whoever reads the scriptures carefully will find, in the Old Testament as well as the New, that it is the definite will of God to have, *on earth*, a people who, in justice and innocence, love not themselves but God and thus become the light for the peoples of earth.

When the time of God comes — the time of the end and of the new beginnings — so it shall be that whatever in Christendom has become tainted and humanized shall suffer merciless collapse, even as Judaism did in the time of Jesus. . . . We must accustom ourselves not to calling Christianity itself the good and the godly, not to taking our confessions and catechisms for the truth. No, the good and the godly, truth and right, are in Christ alone. So it must be all right for the whole of Christendom to collapse, if thereby the good and the godly — namely, Christ — might be revealed as Completer and Fulfiller for all the peoples on earth.

THE CHURCH

"Christianity," as a folk-religion, is headed for ruin.

The time is coming when we will see that, in the outward church, there is a certain "seeking after God" which has something of idol worship about it.

The mind of God for today is not that any human party —even if it be a churchly one — should be the house for which we risk body and soul, which we guard, and for which we pray. It is entirely the other way around. As was the case in ancient Israel, a structure has grown up in Christendom which proceeds from the flesh and does not represent the mind of God. . . . We certainly will not be deceived if, out of present events, we read the mind of God, the mind which leads out of the old system of the rule of the worldly church and into a new and fresh life of truth.

A judgment runs through our time. A finger of truth points to this and that lie or deception in custom and religion. A finger of justice demands that we follow the voice of truth and consider whether everything shouldn't be done differently.

After the human race has continued to live on in tranquility through the centuries, never having been jolted or shaken by the surging waters of history, then all sorts of comfort make themselves at home by way of habit and custom. Finally, these come to be seen as being *of God*. Then it can happen that everything is done only with the consideration of defending human arrangements, because it appears that in these consist the survival of society. It looks as though everything would break apart if these time-bound arrangements were to tumble.

Once a person has made a specialty out of a bad business, he often is too cowardly to hold it up to the judgment of God for *itself* and against *himself*. Thus we can see that a whole lot of nonsense and superstition has crept into Christianity; it is easy enough to spot shortcomings and perversities in our religious institutions. However, people have gotten themselves used to these things and so take them all in stride in order to retain these necessary institutions. So, even though there is much that is perverse and all the people groan under it, still, whenever the righteous voice of God comes, requiring truth and justice, the truth and justice get damned, and the nonsense is defended.

Even *if we were to collect all the good of Christendom and the* church and clothe ourselves in it, the peoples would still remain in darkness. The blackness of sin and death among men and nations is still the typical sign of human existence. In view of this, some people become pessimists and others optimists. However, without the light represented by the actuality of the kingdom of God, neither view has been able to win ascendancy.

The Jesus who says, "I am the truth," is not so revealed in any congregation of Christians that, regarding their manner of life, an observer could with confidence say, "There, in that group, is taking form the truth of God which makes possible the unfolding history of the kingdom of God and allows the goal of the fulfillment of that kingdom to come into sight." ... What we lack is the Holy Spirit, who leads into all truth....

It is no wonder the Holy Spirit is silent when we respect all other spirits more than we do that Spirit. This is why, for a long time, we have taken pains to put ourselves under judgment, in order to become fully conscious as to which we truly prefer: God or the world; Christ or Christendom; church or Spirit.

It is wrong when Christendom allows the life seed of the kingdom of God to remain in its shell, thinking that it should be adored as a mystery. No, it is evident that it must break out at its own time, that it must be *planted* as something which is by nature necessary for the creative process.

Particularly in our own day it has become evident that the kingdom of God does not attach itself to individuals of special piety, to single churches and congregations. Now the world has opened up; and the times display a character enabling us to see that God has not conceived of the world as consisting in individuals but as an entirety. All of today's spiritual development toward the kingdom of God carries this sign. Christianity shall be worldwide; and piety shall be openhearted toward all humanity.

PROTESTANTISM AND CATHOLICISM

We should not think that either the Catholics must become Protestant or the Protestants Catholic. No, it was God who prevented Luther from taking over the whole of Germany. Today this failure of the Reformation is seen as a real evil; many have considered the Reformation unfortunate in that it introduced a kind of religious diversity which admittedly has created great strife and conflict in our fatherland. Nevertheless, it still was out of the goodness of God that the older religious life was not straightway destroyed, that the older tradition also has been preserved. That tradition includes what is good and true. And, on the other hand, the Protestants have not represented the truth of all things; they have incorporated much that is not true. Consequently, God has willed that Protestantism and Catholicism remain standing alongside each other.

God's primary purpose in the Reformation was not simply that a more appropriate Christian viewpoint, or religion, or denomination, arise, under which our religious lives could continue. No, it was rather that new light might come, in deed and in truth a preparation for the coming of the Lord. If I were to add anything further, it is that, for me, the three hundred fifty years of the Reformation have been nothing other than an image of a spiritual renewal which must extend through the entire world, beginning as the light and glory of God over all the peoples of earth until it leads to a revival into a new and godly life.

It is a mistake when, in considering the Reformation, we think only of the establishment of Protestantism, the Evangelical Churches — Lutheran, Reformed, or whatever. The Lord had much greater and extensive intentions for the Reformation. Our long-held understanding, that all the redemptive purposes of God would have to be fulfilled in the Evangelicals, as though no other peoples or churches even existed, as though we were a new Israel which had only to dream egotistically and self-lovingly about herself — that was not right.　　　　(Johann Christoph Blumhardt)

THE NEW AWAKENING AND THE
BLUMHARDTS' CONCEPT OF HOPE

There is no other way to quench the thirst, to end the drought, than through God pouring out his Spirit. There are many in this day and age who no longer want to believe this. Why? Because this would be something out of the ordinary, not fitting into the usual courses of this world. . . . For that reason, it appears too big to most people. But I can't help that; I can't make it any smaller, or think of it as any smaller, than it is. . . .

A stream of the Spirit will come. . . . Only let us await it with confidence! Indeed, a small part of the expectation already was fulfilled in the time of the apostles. . . . Indeed, must it not now be fulfilled on a large scale as it was then on a smaller one? In that first outpouring of the Spirit we had proof that God keeps his word. However, now we need it again. We are a dehydrated people. The thirst is almost killing us; and it is entirely too awful how people are deteriorating both inwardly and outwardly. But now, because we need it again, God will also give it again.

(Johann Christoph Blumhardt)

We must exercise justice and seek it with a whole heart. Then our hearts will call for the Holy Spirit to draw near and rule over us. Today justice is like a trembling sword above us. However, it does not yet fall, in order that we not be shattered. There is rather a waiting to see whether people can be found to whom judgment can be revealed, thereby making a new beginning.

"What should be happening from the human side so that things

again can be better?" To this I can answer nothing other than that, among Christians, there should be more sighing and longing for that which is missing, in general more faith in the Holy Spirit.

However, people let everything stand as though it were good enough just as it is. They act as if nothing more were required of them from above — even as they betray the fact that what they do have was contrived and acquired by study rather than by inspiration. . . . Because an evil race still will not believe, it will let the Savior be the one who destroys, who, in judgment, even now smashes everything into the abyss — this, rather than the one who blesses and whose heart, out of concern for the deliverance of the many, moves him to be the instrument for mediating what otherwise would be the *still-promised* Spirit.

Whoever truly wants to do something should learn to have a heart for the millions, as did Jesus, who, not just in appearance but through his blood, showed a desire to bring reconciliation to the entire world. Those who, out of sympathy with the lament over endless misery on all sides, do themselves sigh, weep, and yearn, seeking in the scriptures an understanding of the Holy Spirit — they are the ones who truly help us toward a better time.   (Johann Christoph Blumhardt)

I *see that you are entirely correct in waiting upon God for your* health. I would say only one other thing: do not weaken yourself with the thought that, because you are not yet well, you must be guilty. One can always reproach himself about many things; but it is not good when a person makes the action of God dependent upon his own doing or not doing — especially when someone like you has his whole heart and longing centered upon the authority and help of God. Only remain firm in your love for God, even when the move out of disease and into life and health goes slowly. You are and will remain God's; and you can continually come to know that in your heart.

All *sick people should note this: God cannot save when guilt is* present; he is just. This has been clear to me for many years;

there has never been a time when I could simply pray, "May the people become healthy." No, for a long time I have known very well that, under the circumstances, help does not come through the prayer, "Make me well," but rather through the patient word, "I will suffer." Often, through suffering, one must do a kindness for our dear God, as it were. The more a person will, gladly and entirely, go to meet him, the more that which is lacking can be made whole.

Signs and wonders are all right as legitimate proof that one has to do with our dear God; but they cannot truly help us. What helps us is justice and truth; and a hundred thousand miracles are of little use in comparison to one word of truth, or one command of truth through which God makes something straight that was crooked.

A great many prayers and sighs climb clear up to heaven and then fall back to earth again like the rain. Very few penetrate to the throne of God so that it can be said, "They have been prayed."

If I do not have an ear to the telephone in order to receive from God into myself, then likewise God does not have an ear on the other end to receive my words into himself. God will not hear us one-sidedly; there must be correspondence between us.

Thus, it is understandable that sometimes it must be said to people, "Suspend all your praying for a time! Seek first to receive God into yourselves, be fair to him; and then prayer will come of itself without forethought. It will be childlike and in accordance with the truth."

From our side, the first thing is that we listen to God. However, if, in our inward being, we are open only to the next best, the bustle of the world, then in earthly pleasures and afflictions our hearts are roused for our own sakes. Then, if the uplifting God does not make us uplifted, we may be sure that our praying is not actually prayer. God can well hear the sighs of everyone, even the foolish; yet, in reality, only those can pray who listen to God.

HOW DOES THE KINGDOM
OF GOD COME?

GIFT AND TASK: WAITING AND WORKING

That which is of God is ready at all times; but the question is whether *you* are ready for *it*.

God makes use of us. We must not want to make use of Jesus for ourselves but must want Jesus to make use of us, must want to give ourselves entirely to his use.

It is wholly proper that we earthly people put in an appearance before God. We are part of God's creation; and it is a matter of sorrow in heaven when nobody comes in the Spirit, bowing in adoration before him. For God, that is grief, because he loves the world.

Christ takes his stand in a very high domain, to which he would draw us. Not everybody can manage it, for those who would go to Jesus must see all things in a high light and yet not be afraid to take the distress and need of mankind upon themselves. Only when we will move into the deep misery of mankind, where so many hearts are bleeding, can we break the new road up to Jesus.

Must it be only out of goodness and not from any need that God employs someone? That is exactly as if a person should say that a father has no need that his sons help him; it is only goodness when he simply allows them, as his children, to come on their own. As if it could make no difference to a father whether his sons desert him and he has to hire outsiders!

But all that is nothing. We do not even want to stay with the Father simply as servants. No, then it would be preferable that, like the prodigal son, we waste in riotous living the wealth which the Father gave us, until we land with the pigs. Then, naturally, it must be an honor for the Father when we return home in rags—although, certainly, we should not be as stupid as the prodigal, who wanted to work and be a day-laborer. No, we come only to be blessed in that very coming!

Once in a while God needs people who will help him. That is the secret of the summons into covenant; without the covenant with God, nothing happens. I know very well what is regularly hurled at me: "We can't *build* the kingdom of God." Obviously not; we cannot build it; and it is just for that reason the Almighty founded a covenant. Through it, he would have people who bear fruit for him, who fight for him, who no longer misuse weapons upon human flesh but use them to carve out of the evil, blasphemous world of men that which will be to God's honor, that it might be great. For this, God needs people. Yet many are called, but few are chosen. Why is this? Because they do not truly give themselves; and when they are called, they still can't be used.

Mark this well: The kingdom of God takes shape through nothing other than the coming of the Lord. It is not formed through any human discovery, no matter how worthy and honorable. ... Yet it is remarkable that, for all of this, not only God, the creator of the heavens, but also *men* must be in on the plan. But this makes sense. For if there were no people at all involved, but only God, then truly it would have to be said that man was *not* created in the image of God. Nevertheless, man *shall* be in the image of God and shall remain so; as such, he shall become the co-worker of God in the most great and most holy work of that which God purposes for his creation.

Through the whole life of the Savior we see his desire to find faith among people on earth. It is as though, without this faith, that which he has in mind could not come to be. We could say that the Savior, on the one side, places his trust in his Father in heaven; yet, on the other side, he places it in people also, as those to whom something from the Father has been given. People put their faith in Jesus; and out of this faith he sees, thriving and growing, the work of God which shall bring his kingdom to its glorious end.

THE LITTLE FLOCK

Meanwhile, God does not need much upon earth. He needs only a few yet *total* persons; he can lay hold of these few, so to say, and by them the whole world can be held firm. Do not consider yourselves too insignificant, dear friends. Leave behind the ordinary disposition of people who think that there must always be large masses representing the kingdom of God on earth. It is much better when we are a little band. One, two, three, ten people who are united are stronger than a hundred thousand who thrash about in their piety yet never arrive at a true and unanimous striving for the kingdom of God.

This light [i.e., the hope of a new heaven and a new earth] would not deceive anyone. In it, you may remain a little rascal; but it is the greatest folly to believe that we must straight-way become the greatest heroes. God always works through *weak* people. Yet they are the strongest, because in them, through the Spirit's power, hope can be most effective.

Things were very dark for the disciples of Jesus, because they did not see in him any power by which he could make people subject to him. He was always the weak one — the poor one among the poor, the despised one among the despised — and he didn't lift a finger to create any sort of importance for himself. . . . In the world, one is used to seeing only strong people making something of themselves, people who understand how to take power into their own hands; but he was always the weak one. The Lord Jesus was not the sort of man who would say to his disciples, "Pay attention to how I bring things off. The future is mine!" No, he refused all this and came to nothing — in *this* world, perhaps we should say.

In every age, whatever is difficult is understood only by a few. That to which everyone runs; that which everyone, as part of the herd, simply accepts — that is easy. So, not where the many dash and run, but where only a few are to be seen — there lies the deeper truth. And so today Jesus' "little flock" consists of those who are not content with run-of-the-mill Christianity but who trust in one who is greater, having hope in a high goal for mankind.

Dear friends, God can help through just a few people and through our hope, which is the Spirit. The Spirit is greater than the whole world. The children of God depend upon the Holy Spirit; and the Holy Spirit enters them and makes of them a dwelling of God so that from just one sighing child of God the entire glory of God can radiate. God does not need to count and say, "Yes, by all means I must have a hundred thousand in the world; otherwise nothing will succeed; if there are only a thousand, then all is lost." Such calculation is not necessary for God. If he has only several — indeed, at present, hardly any — yet through one person he can let such glory radiate that the hope gleams through the whole world.

Our dear God never lets his little flock become prominent. They are always in the background. They might be ever so successful and strong within themselves; but they will never win human fame through human deeds, not even if they be the finest of prophets or angels. Indeed, precisely because they are such, they must remain hidden. Our dear God is not about to strike a deal with mankind on the basis of any great personages he can claim for himself. . . .

Not the strong and powerful, but the simple, the insignif-icant, the ones the world doesn't count, those who face great difficulties without apparent help but who yet have a place within them where God can rule — these are the ones through whom God will accomplish his purpose, whether they be men or women, the children or the aged, the foolish or the clever. None of this depends upon our intellect or strength but upon the rule of God.

Until Jesus comes, his will remain a "little flock." Yet this is not simply because only a little flock are to be called to glory — oh, what an awful mistake! no! no! — it is because the rest of the poor people simply have not the wherewithal to bring off the assignment. . . . But the little flock arrives at the goal; and it is through this flock that the kingdom will be given. . . .

Before this time, the kingdom remains a matter only for individuals, but thereafter, for all. Then shall they be retrieved from the hells and the depths, from sin and from death. Sin and death shall not have won a single person. This is a freedom we have in God; we will be able to stand so firmly that not a single hell will be able to say, "This man belongs to me." "No, he belongs to God," I say; and if no one else will say it, I do. Not a single hell can say, "The man is mine." No, no! Either all belong to my Father in heaven or else none do.

If I must give up hope for any person in any respect, then Jesus is not risen. I tell you this before God and his angels, before Jesus himself, "You are not the light of the world if I have to give up hope." . . . For me, this *is* the resurrection of Jesus Christ.

Of course, it takes a real battle to keep oneself within this light of redemption, because I must ever create this redeemed world within myself, as it were. We always stand in psychological, spiritual, and physical relationships to the world as a whole. And now one sees all and feels all; when one is thus transformed by the light of the resurrection, there is pain, but it has an end. There are hells; but they have an end. There is death and sin enough; but they will reach their ends.

In this knowledge, I can bear the pain; it is integral to justice that there be reward *and punishment*, grace *and judgment*. As long as good and evil are operating simultaneously, then it is a necessary part of justice that these things exist — even if only temporarily.

But before you come to faith — the faith that hell, sin, and death have an end; that all people are God's; that, if we believe in Jesus Christ, we are to fight in behalf of all people — before we can promote the love of God in heaven, under the earth, and in all people; before we can ourselves become realized persons in eternal life — before any of this, we believers have to fight against melancholy, a melancholy that is laid directly upon *us*. However, we must not, to the world, be an example of mourning. If we cannot rejoice in our faith, then we cannot invite other people into it. So we must put the pain behind us and hold firmly and steadily to the Lord, placing heaven and earth under their master.

Because God has made us great, so that we cannot be satisfied with small things, so we must also learn to think big. If you can believe me, throw off the shackles; think big! The hellish gospel, the devil's gospel, must be trodden under foot so that, in the end, Jesus can come to all creatures and no false prophet can make difficult the path of my soul to the Father in heaven.

My beloved friends, the one who does this is *Jesus*!

THE PEOPLE OF GOD AND THE SERVICE OF GOD

There should always be a people gathered on the basis of revelation, of whom God can say, "You are *my* people." To these, his people, great promises regarding both earthly and eternal life are given. And the promise has been maintained in the revelation of God even into the new age, the age of Jesus Christ. Also, in the name of Jesus Christ, a community shall be founded in which everything

God has promised shall come to fulfillment. Today it is the fellowship of the Holy Spirit that produces the community for which the promises are intended.

It so happens that there is only a very small band of those who truly want to be *fighters*. I tell you, there are *peoples*, Christian peoples, where not a single person is a fighter, not one. There are thousands of *Christians*, and *not one* will hazard his blood; they all make excuses. . . . They bow and scrape around the Lord Jesus, but they are not fighters. They will not give their lives even unto death; and whoever will not do so can never be a disciple of Jesus, fighting for his victory.

Until all sin is checked, until the darknesses which have accumulated for centuries are dissolved and removed from among people, the community of Christ must suffer. Yet, thanks be to God, in this suffering we also discover a help that makes it possible to hold out. . . . We who believe in the Savior can legitimately think of ourselves as people who, through our own suffering, help in the suffering of Jesus Christ by which the darkness is overcome. Insofar as we are thinking of other people, our suffering becomes a force which helps the Father in heaven in building his kingdom on earth. . . . The cross of Jesus led to the resurrection; and our cross will also bring resurrection. . . . Those who bear their crosses are Jesus' co-workers, working to make all things new.

It is possible that the fruit of our prayers will first be experienced by later generations, by generations breaking forth in the songs of praise which we ourselves would have liked to address to heaven in thanks for the *granting* of those prayers. Yet, how many attacks does it take before the walls of a well-entrenched city are breached? Our prayers, it might be said, are hammer-strokes against the bulwark of the princes of darkness; they must be oft repeated. Many years can pass by, even a number of generations die away, before a breakthrough occurs. However, not a single hit is wasted; and if they are continued, then even the most secure wall must finally fall. Then the glory of the Lord will have a clear path upon which to stride forth with healing and blessing for the wasted fields of mankind. (Johann Christoph Blumhardt)

THE ZION OF GOD

What is Zion, and who is "the inhabitant of Zion" who is said to "shout and sing for joy" (Isa. 12:6)? It is the personality who, according to God's revelation, dies to the world and lives for God. Sometimes it has been only one person who could shout and sing for joy because he was allowed an experience of the living God. Often it has been several, an entire community; it could be thousands or even millions. The more people it is, the more pleasing it is to our dear God. But Zion must be a sort of people who are so fired by the light and life of God that they give themselves body and soul, making God the single treasure of their hearts, cost what it may. . . . Zion is not an earthly faction, not a community possessing mere religious teachings and forms. The true people of Zion have no particular artistic or technical skill, no strength of character that would make them persons of importance. Their strength is in God alone. . . . These people are "the inhabitant of Zion."

Whenever, upon earth, God's cause was to take a step forward, then God always created a Zion, i.e., a smaller or larger community of people differentiated by their manner of life, with hearts kept open to God's doing and speaking. Apart from such a Zion, there has never been anything of God's splendor given to the world. Out of a Zion, for the first time, come rights and laws which are themselves right, living, and true; without such a Zion, they die off and become a dead weight on the body of humanity.

Godly truth and eternity can dwell upon earth only so far as there is created what we call a "Zion," in which people pay attention to these things.

85

THE INVISIBLE BATTLEFIELD

Because our human world displays increasing activity in its resistance to God, there is a battle. It is a battle taking place primarily in inwardness, in the invisible life-impulses of man. However, the expectation is that, once the invisible has been swept clear of all hindrance, then visible change also can show itself in clear and true manifestations of life. . . . If, through the stirring and moving of their lives toward the truth, the people of God achieve victory over this unjust and untrue interior existence, then the out-ward — as far as this age will allow — can immediately be formed as new, true, and eternal.

There is a battle taking place outside of human society. There is a battle taking place in the spiritual regions surrounding us. There is, on the one side, the bright, clear light of God which presses toward people, allowing them to lift themselves from the ground to experience new spiritual development time and again, to come, time and again, to moral growth and achievement — all of this being the great and mighty working of the good in the midst of humanity. . . . And on the other side, there is always the enemy of the good and of mankind, the enemy of God and his people.

BAD BOLL, A ZION OF GOD

Here at Bad Boll I *have not cared to emphasize the fact that I* actually am a *parson.* Simply as a *housefather*, I have more freedom of movement. . . . So I have decided to remove from my person everything of a churchly character. . . . I believe that, here at Boll, regarding those matters with which we essentially are concerned, still truer ways will develop. In particular, we do not want simply to learn the churchly conduct of gatherings and sermons. No, in our daily life we want to learn how to be out meeting the kingdom of God in order, thus, to make our way into the will of God. . . .

Among us, that shall not be called "worship" which, through words and thoughts, seeks merely an elevation to spiritual heights. Rather, the illumination of hearts in body-life and the burning struggle there where living takes place — this, as a testimony to the honor of God, is what we would call "worship." . . . In Bad Boll we are founding not another *preaching* station, but a *living* station. . . . Let us live with one another. And most important, let us climb from the spiritual heights down to the completely simple ground of life. . . . All the circumstances of our day cry, not for preaching and rhetorical deluge, but for examples of the good, examples of the truth.

Today *someone wrote to tell me that, at their house, Bad Boll is* called "The Island of the Blessed." That very much touched my heart; and I thought, "Yes, if only it were so!" . . . We don't have any special teachings and don't offer any special rites; but we do want to be a people of blessedness. All who come here should sense something blessed among us. At least, it is to this end I would like to be a servant of God.

THE HUMAN VISION

When we look back over the history of mankind, we see a forest where trees once grew but where the storms have passed, laying it waste. In this, in the whole unhappy course of mankind, our dear God is still the manager who allows people — who must belong to *him* — to be his saints. These are people in whom he is a power and to whom he simply says, "You must go my way and demonstrate that, even under evil conditions, a way is to be found which can be traveled without becoming entangled." . . . Always, when things are to move forward, God must have saints who also stand in their own times; who understand the times; who know how to live among the people of the times; but who, even though the times be ever so perverted, still carry the high thoughts of the kingdom of God in their spirits.

There are at hand battles against evil that must be carried through. God assigns these battles to us; and for that reason we must not think that things always have to go well with us. Our existence is justified only if we will fight against evil and make a pact with the good against the evil. . . . That, at a future time, this battle will resolve itself into a victory in which we can rejoice — that is our consolation. For the present, however, the battle itself is our joy. And even when the going gets hot, we will remain loyal in battle — that is our calling. It is because the *entire* human race is not in a position to do so that God entrusts this battle to particular individuals, individuals who can intercede on behalf of everyone.

What I see as the greatest danger for most people is that of judging themselves and others against a norm set up by society, one by which people can flatter themselves. And this self-justification becomes a powerful force. As a stance before God, it is colossal autonomy. In that situation, one dare not raise any questions about the encompassing social milieu.

Ultimately, however, the *only* thing of importance is God's opinion. Men can neither justify nor damn; only God can. . . . To be able to live *before him* — this is what we must seek. We don't need the slightest recognition from men; and we don't want it, either. We need only God's recognition on earth. His freedom, nobility, and superiority must captivate us. I do not want to be dependent upon anything else, so that I can be completely dependent upon God, his eternity, truth, and greatness.

W*e should be in high humor all the day, strong in spirit, vigorous,* godly, powerful against all enemies and the hindrances of life.

N*o cursing, no ill will, no contempt ever should be heard from our* mouths; this is the new — perhaps brand-new — attitude which can work inconspicuously in our time. We have been prohibited from heaping hatred on our enemies, even when we have been totally misunderstood. Today it is *this* enemy-loving Jesus who has become great, in whom we are able to bear all enmity with hearts full of blessing.

WORK, DISAPPOINTMENT, AND FULFILLMENT

When I see people as they are, when they are building things higher and higher, when they are aroused against all that is evil — I always see also that they will soon fall away, exhausted and sick. The weeds choke them; they don't have the breath of God; they think that, by external means, they can do what needs to be done; the breath of God has gone out of them.

Thus, our situation always would be hopeless, if it weren't that we have a great hope: the Lord sends reapers into the harvest first to clear out the weeds (Matt. 13:24– 30). For me, this represents the most heartfelt need of our times. These reapers, we should know, are not men, not visible men. We could not possibly do this job. No one should think that he is able to loosen the weeds from any other person. He always will destroy the grain itself; and weeds look to him like good grain.

The weeds are actually people's desire for reputation one over another — envy, jealousy, and all. Yet all the greater is that which the Lord Jesus sees and proclaims and to which he also opens our eyes. There are the reapers whom the Lord very quietly sends into the harvest. These are invisible powers, including his Holy Spirit and his angels. These are all the million-faceted powers of the good which God has given. The time is coming when they will receive a knife in their hands; and the enemy of God and of men will be deprived of his fruit.

Regarding that which the Lord is waiting to bring together for the first time, in quiet and obscurity God already has done a very great deal. The eternal God can create at the deepest, most hidden levels that which no human being notices. In fact, he creates much that, if our eyes were opened to see, would truly amaze us. . . . Indeed, on the surface it can look as though there were no God in heaven. Yet none of us sees into the depths; and God does not intend that we should be able to. Yet, if we are awaiting something — a new age, a time of redemption — then we dare not assume that this possibly would come overnight, without preparation.   (Johann Christoph Blumhardt)

DANGER OF DEGENERACY

(Areas in which Blumhardt's thought might become distorted among his followers)

BEING QUIET OR QUIETISM?

The hope derived from the light of the Holy Spirit also has its reverse side, namely, that we come alive and recognize that the hope itself is alive with possibilities for us — possibilities, we should say, that lie in God, certainly, but in the creation as well. There are people who think nothing more is possible than what they can see with their half-dead eyes. Thus, when they hope, it is a feeble matter, because they always think, "We can't do anything at all; everything must come down from heaven."

It is different with those who know true hope; they become active on their own. How can I hope for a new heaven and a new earth in which justice dwells, how can I hope out of the strength of the Spirit, unless I am conducting myself in such a way that something more just, something better, *can* be created on earth? For everything God does must happen through us. It would be wrong for us to do nothing at all. As soon as God lays some promise in our hearts — and he has laid it in our hearts that things shall be better — in his doing this, there also comes a certain strength: "Now begin! The hope is there; so you can begin!"*

---

*As in an earlier instance, Ragaz's personal predilection here again seems to have biased his choice of Blumhardt quotations. His heading has it exactly right in implying that "being quiet" is something different from "quietism." He is right, too, in suggesting that there is the *danger* that, among his followers, Blumhardt's position could *degenerate* into a "quietism."

However, Ragaz's own bent may have blinded him to the fact that there is just as great a *danger* that Blumhardt's position could *degenerate* into a humanistic, self-confident "activism." The full truth of Blumhardt will be better served if we supplement the Ragaz quotation by putting it into tension with these — again, taken from the Lejeune book, *Christoph Blumhardt and His Message*, pp. 77 – 78:

"Waiting is a great strength. Waiting is a great deed."

"Let us arise in the knowledge that a Christian is a helper in this hope, full of the strength of waiting."

"Truly waiting people, true Christians who wait for the day of God's mercy upon all men, may gently spin the thread and twine it around the nations, tying them to our faith and preserving them for the day of Jesus Christ. What a coming of Christ that would be if many Christians were to say, 'I too want to do something, I want to be a strength in quiet, through my waiting for the sake of others.' "

I *would say that, in a certain sense, it is a deception when Christians* seek peace — if they understand peace as though, through the gospel, a comfortable life should be made for them. The opposite is the case. The verse is relevant here: "I have not come to bring peace, but a sword" (Matt. 10:34). We have peace as long as the battle endures — but only *in the battle*. A soldier has peace when the bullet hits him and he falls dead, *as an honorable fighter in the war*. A soldier does not have peace when he lies in his tent sleeping through the fighting.

FREEDOM OR FORMULA?

The *love of God makes free. We always have been free people, for* we stand in the love of God. And I say to you, dear friend,

"Wherever you may be, if you succeed in saying 'Jesus' in such way that everything of your own falls to the ground and you come into the love of the Father, then you are free."

The regime of God requires free people. . . . God needs flexible people; in the love of God we are uncommonly flexible. And in direct correlation to the needs of the kingdom of God we must be ready to change; we cannot continue century after century in *one* manner.

God *meets me in a completely different way than he does you.* All of us may have the same concept of Yahweh; but he will never speak to you as he does to me; he will appear individually to you differently from what he does to me. There remains a certain freedom in every individual regarding our feeling for God and our relationship to him — even though we are united as *one* people through *one* Spirit. Yahweh is nothing mechanistic.

I *cannot say more than that I would that everyone might be placed* here, where *we* are weak, in order that, together, we could experience the kingdom of God. You should not say, "I am something, and *you* are nothing; you must become as I am!" — which generally is the way Christians relate to one another. . . . But the closer you are to the kingdom of God, the more gentle and humble, the more simple you will become. Christ will become your life. . . . Be meek, and thus Christ will rule.

The *world will be captured for the kingdom of heaven without* proselytism. In time, the conversion will happen of itself; the more the rule of God becomes part of *us*, the more the eyes of others will be opened. . . . The more we succeed in accepting all of God, all of Jesus, all of the Holy Spirit, the more the world will become enlightened. . . .

At this point, Christians understand the word of Jesus in an entirely false way: "Go forth into all the world!" Do your going into the world in the greatest sense; but conversion is not your business. It doesn't even occur to the Lord Jesus to commission us to convert people!... If the Spirit of God does not do the converting, we had just as well put our cause on the shelf. There is something so high and yet so hidden in human beings, something so exclusively the property of the Father in heaven, that, when it is ready to break free, our fumbling hands and coarse sense dare not interfere with the secret fabric of a human soul.

Jesus wants a people who will bring forth the good and yet leave the bitterest adversary his freedom.

HEARTS OR HEADS?

Don't believe that we can accomplish anything toward the furtherance of God's goal unless we, in some way, become honestly centered in him alone. Every other consideration is a matter of indifference. It is completely unimportant what, otherwise, we have in the way of "thoughts." We want to be prepared for *him*, because, in the end, it is the person of Christ that makes the difference and not some teaching from him or about him. In the meantime, then, we must look into the invisible and cry, "Jesus!" That is not so easy to do — that is, if one does it *without "thoughts."* With "thoughts," it *is* easy.

Very many people come to me, all crying, "Jesus!" — but with thoughts. I first have to make them "thoughtless," because, in their calling to Jesus, they are laying down certain conditions, even though all unconsciously. They are calling for a Jesus of a particular color, so to speak. One person likes the color "pietism" and so wants only the pietist Jesus. Another prefers "churchliness" and wants the Jesus of that color. Thus, human preferences and thoughts set themselves up above Jesus himself.... When it comes to what people would rather have, whether Jesus or their own thoughts about him, they will fight to the death for their own thoughts....

With the help of theological systems and convictions, anybody can call, "Jesus!" If a person can't do it for himself, he attaches himself to a teacher and, in the name of this teacher, calls, "Jesus!" But, without reserve, to have it that Jesus is Master, because he comes from God, that happens but seldom. ... Yet, where someone calls, "Jesus," because that is what he perceives; where someone slips out of his human achievement, out of that into which he was born, out of what has become historical custom; where someone calls, "Jesus," and calls in faith — there wonders happen, there something flashes down from heaven, there one is overwhelmed by the holy.

It is not upon our thoughts that all depends but upon our hearts. The final outcome of religion must be simple enough that all can understand it.

Everyone must concede that the kingdom of God comes not through logical concepts but through surprises.

Jesus gives us no religion, no philosophy or morals — he gives us power.

If the gospel were served only by us parsons, if it had to be maintained only by human wisdom from the pulpits of the learned, then it would have died long ago. Truly I say to you, it never comes to the place that things depend upon our knowing something scientific about Christianity or our remembering particular principles of faith and morals. ... No, it is not that. The essence of Christianity is not to be found in our understanding. Rather, it is there where simple hearts are awakened time and again, there where resurrected people are present, the inexplicable ones for which science hasn't even words. If it were not for these joyous, faithful people, often coming from the lowest strata of society, then the gospel would die.

OUTLOOK AND TASK

[It was in the Fall of 1914
that Blumhardt spoke these words.]

Before peace can come, there is much darkness that must be overcome.
... When that has happened, then it shall be said, "He comes!
Our dear God has answered our hope in him and our understand-
ing with him by again giving peace.".... Thus we can rejoice —
right now, in these troubled times. At least I am rejoicing, for
I am certain that the living God is doing something among us.
Following this sad time, a new grace will arise from him who is
there and who was there and who will be there.

The entire history of the community of Jesus Christ has
proven this: time and again, after the most sorrowful times, when
one has believed that everything is going to smash, all at once
our dear God is again there with his powerful help.... With
you, I groan before God over the outbreak of the grievous events
annihilating humanity. Yet these circumstances have come from
God and are holy; there must be a transformation of all things.

God's ways lead through judgment; and that judgment must
create good. A cleansing shall take place in our unclean society;
and the word of God shall remain our light and comfort even in
the death of an age and its culture. The kingdom of God will
now be prepared in earnest; and I rejoice that, in his earnestness,
God is now speaking with mankind. This is itself a grace which
remains firm in our hearts. Trouble and the works of men will
pass away. God's grace and the victory over sin, death, and hell
will become fact even in our time.

The last times very likely will be troubled in that, as the past perishes, a great mass of people will arise wanting to defend the behavior of their false persons and to gather the worshippers of that past. . . . It is written, "Then if anyone says to you, 'Lo, here is the Christ!' or 'There he is!' do not believe it" (Matt. 24:23).

We see, then, how certain cultivated religious causes will arise, claiming that Christ has become lost, when, in actuality, it is only the causes themselves that have become lost, i.e., very simply, *they* must disappear. For here lies a secret, namely, that until these false Christs are silenced, the true Christ will not let himself be heard *aloud*. You may believe that for certain. Yet we must also live through times when Christ is lost — and we must not cry for him to reveal himself clearly to the world. One must be sensible when one prays; today I would not at all want the Savior to join the cryings in the wilderness. Against the last shrieks of irrational religiosity, as they now echo through Christendom, we must plug our ears and look on serenely while these causes die. One day they *must* die; and until they have died, Christ cannot make his voice audible.

We are convinced that in this time, when everything is being ruined and broken, inconspicuous seeds of the kingdom of God yet are being planted in the world. These seeds, which come from God himself, will not rot under the debris of the present-day world but will much more truly, while the old is being rolled out of the way, grow upwards to serve as a transfiguration of the name "Jesus" to "The Christ of the World."

Therefore, let as much torment and grief take root here and there among people as will, we will not despair but rather look to the future with courage, not letting ourselves become dependent upon this or that law or human order but letting ourselves be dependent upon Jesus, the light of the world. He will live and conquer until the entire creation glistens with his light to the glory of God, until our race of men who have ever been lost finally find the path which alone will lead them to the goal, to the destiny which, as sons of God, they have in creation.

CONCLUSION

We in the final battle stand,
Where Life and Death are fighting.
Remain, then, under God's command,
If wrong you would be righting.
The world, the old, is overthrown;
And Jesus' kingdom, it alone,
Arises from the ruins.

part two

JOHN REGEHR is Associate Professor of Practical Theology at Mennonite Brethren Bible College, Winnipeg, Canada. In 1970, he completed his doctorate at Southern Baptist Theological Seminary with a dissertation, *The Preaching of Christoph Blumhardt*. As source material for that study, Regehr translated thirty-one talks and sermons out of the collected works of the younger Blumhardt. Ultimately, Regehr's committee decided that the translations should not be incorporated as part of the dissertation itself; so they have not been published in any form.

We have selected sixteen of those pieces to constitute Part Two of this volume. With the idea of getting as much of Blumhardt into English as possible, first Regehr and subsequently we ourselves deliberately have chosen items that do not duplicate what is available from Plough Publishing House. With only minor editing, the translation that follows is Regehr's and is used with his permission.

In no way will these sermons serve as a substitute for what Ragaz accomplished in Part One. Nevertheless, they do carry a particular advantage of their own. Here, by reading complete presentations rather than excerpts, we can get a better "feel" for Blumhardt the teacher and preacher, for his style and the impact of his presence. Part One *plus* Part Two imparts to us much more of Blumhardt than either could do on its own.

Regehr arranged his selections in the chronological order of their original delivery; I have chosen, instead, to form them into a somewhat logical sequence. In the interest of including as much of Blumhardt's thought as possible, I also have taken the liberty to condense and to excerpt where that seemed helpful.

The appendix at the back of the book identifies each piece as to source and date and indicates what sort of editing has been done. Unless otherwise indicated, the quotations of scripture are from the Revised Standard Version.

THE NAME JESUS

And at the end of eight days, when he was circumcised,
he was called Jesus, the name given by the angel before he was
conceived in the womb. (Luke 2:21)

He came as the little child over whom the angels sang jubilantly, "Glory to God in the highest, and on earth peace among men with whom he is pleased." Upon being given the name Jesus, he stepped into the ranks of those who are called and known by name. And in this action God revealed himself in a particular way for the salvation of mankind.

This is not a name which men are inclined to give their children, but it is the name which the Father in heaven gives to a son of man. By that name the Father designates him as *his* Son and introduces him to us as *our* brother. It is a name by which the Father in heaven wants to say something to us and through which he wants to create something.

The name Jesus means Savior, Redeemer. The Father calls this, his Son, Savior, and makes him our brother in order that he might say to us, "You shall be saved!"

In every age, the greatest darkness among people has been that they have lost the light of their life and consequently have not been able to look to the future with prospects of life. Indeed, it has always been the torment of people not to know with certainty their ultimate destiny. But because the Father in heaven names the newborn child Jesus, every person knows whom he can count on concerning his life: "You shall be saved!" And now if you want to be a genuine person, you can be so if only, from the name Jesus, you read the announcement that the Father in heaven has made it his purpose to save you and all mankind. In the name of Jesus, the Savior, the Father wants to bring people into certainty regarding their salvation. And the name of Jesus not only *proclaims* this salvation, it *creates* it. . . .

If the name Jesus is to communicate such an understanding to us, then each individual will have to make an effort to keep the understanding alive in himself. It is not wholesome for you to permit doubts about what God wants to do with you. It is a transgression against the name Jesus when you doubt that God wants to save you. Don't be misled, you who have heard the gospel and have been instructed in all that God has done through the Savior for the blotting out of your sins. Don't be misled when the world preaches something else or when your experience in the world seems an attempt to convince you that God is really not much concerned about your life. Assert the truth; you can know it and do know it, "I am being saved." This is the first sermon that comes from Jesus. You are being saved; be assured of that! . . .

We must be firm in this — that, once the Lord Jesus has grasped us by his word, we understand him according to the word: "For God so loved the world . . . that whoever believes in him should not perish but have eternal life." If you have laid hold on that, and if you know that Jesus Christ was born, that he died for your sins; if you know that he was raised and is seated at the right hand of the Father — then know this, too, that you are being saved. The name Jesus proclaims this to you. . . .

Though there be confusion in my life, "I am being saved nonetheless." Though sins still break into my life, "Nevertheless, I am being saved." Though hell assail me and the devil attack me, "Still I am being saved." We have a confidence; and we affirm it against the flesh, the world, the devil and hell, against everything that may be named: "We are being saved, because Jesus has come." This we know; it has been told us in the name Jesus by the Father in heaven himself. We don't merely suppose it; we *know* it. The truth that we are being saved is one of the fundamental facts laid into our understanding in the name Jesus. . . .

But more, beloved. Not concerning ourselves only are we to know that we are being saved — indicating, perhaps, to others, "We don't know about you." Not only are we forbidden to express condemnation regarding others, we must not even become indifferent regarding those who do not yet appear to have been seized by the gospel as we have been. We must not become uncertain in our thinking about the world, about the souls of people in general. The most certain truth in the Bible is that God wants to save all of mankind, indeed all of creation.

If Jesus is named Jesus, and if he thus is proclaimed to be sent by the Father and born a man and, at the same time, is proclaimed as the firstborn of all creation and the eternal word of God in whom all that lives has its life, then there must lie in this name Jesus — the name voiced by God, the name which is the Alpha and the Omega of creation — there must lie in this name the proclamation that the whole of creation is being saved. Our loving God wants to carry the proclamation of salvation *into the world*; and in this "Jesus-age" in which we are living, we may regard every person with a view to his salvation and may instruct him concerning the same.

Once we have received into our spirits this proclamation of the name Jesus — I'd like to call it "the Creation-Proclamation" — then we become even more full of light. We already have a certain measure of light when assured of our own salvation, we who have been laid hold of by the gospel. But we become much more resplendent and more powerful — in other words, more "apostolic" — when we accept the understanding that the name Jesus assures salvation for all creatures, regardless of who they are, regardless of what they do, regardless of what kind of life it is in which they find themselves. Jesus — named by God the Father — makes the proclamation of the gospel reliable, makes the announcing of salvation for all creation valid. And we may view the lost from this perspective. . . .

It is my opinion that the further the times advance and the more we see the powers of sin and unbelief and of death and hell entangling people and seeking to draw them away from the proclamation of the gospel, so much the more must we establish in ourselves the conviction that God has set salvation as his goal. Just that much more must we gain courage to set ourselves against these devils of our time and contest the prey they already have taken. . . .

We do not want to regard as gospel that which we can mutter sleepily, as Eli did, "May the Lord do what pleases him." No, we want to oppose such spiritlessness and stand in the gap as Moses did. If Moses, that servant of God, could wrest from the name of God mercy and grace, patience and faithfulness, for the entire people of Israel—then we can have the same courage (with the same repentance, of course) to announce the gospel, which is the will of God *for salvation*. This is the message we want to proclaim against the devil, against all the powers of hell, against all the evil in the world which accuses and condemns mankind: "You will not win out! This we know because we know Jesus. You must vacate the world." Mankind belongs to God and to Jesus Christ; and salvation will not be denied to this groaning world.

Jesus is the firstborn of all creation; he is the firstborn from the dead; and it has pleased God that in him all the fullness of God should dwell, and through him to reconcile to himself all things, whether on earth or in heaven, making peace by the blood of his cross [a paraphrase of Colossians 1:15 – 20]. The incarnation of Christ is his union with *all* flesh, with all humanity; and if God calls this one who is united with all flesh "Jesus," then *salvation* is thereby proclaimed to all flesh. And we must avail ourselves of this truth if the name Jesus is to bear full weight on our understanding. . . .

Be serious about "condemnation" for a moment. If those sitting next to you are to be deprived of salvation because of *their* present condition, then how much of *your own* being would have to go down into hell as well? Or do you suppose that exceptions will be made for certain people? Such a procedure would never even occur to God; he is righteous. Therefore, *for our own sake* we must hold fast the proclamation of salvation *for all*.

In this, I do not wish to say that, at the end of time, God cannot and may not make a separation. What decisions must be made at the last judgment and what will happen to those who up to that time have not been saved — all that is *his* business. I say only this: Now, in our time, as long as God has not passed down his ultimate decision, the task has been given us to carry into the consciousness of all people the name Jesus, the name that is significant because it promises *salvation*. And we are to anticipate that salvation with sympathetic, priestly seriousness. . . .

Now we want to touch on a further truth which the name Jesus proclaims. We have in him not only *the concept of* salvation but also *the power of God for* salvation. Not only does the name of Jesus *proclaim* salvation, but it is Jesus who *creates* it. Consequently, the gospel is called a power of salvation to all who believe it, who really want to be saved — by Jesus. We must not despair even though the world continues long under the *proclamation* of salvation without actually attaining it. We must not despair even though we ourselves, often in the face of intense salvation-preaching, see no instant redemption from sin and death. We must not despair because of the delay of the thorough-going redemption which is proclaimed in Jesus. In the name of Jesus, the world has been brought into safety by the Father in heaven — initially through the *announcement* of all-encompassing redemption but ultimately through the promised *entry* of salvation in the second coming of Jesus Christ. . . .

Our community would long since have ceased to exist if we did not know and affirm Jesus as the power of God, as the victor. We would long since have been lost if, likewise, we did not see this Jesus invade our lives against ourselves, against the malicious trickery of our hearts, against the half-commitment of our faith, against the sluggishness of our being, and against our worldliness that persistently keeps surfacing.

Often we have had to wait for years to see any improvement in something in which destruction had already taken root.

We could then have done what many do in view of destruction. They say, "We must simply let it take its course; that's the way human life is." No! no! We let nothing "run its course"! We must know Jesus as the power of God which is able to rescue in any situation — and not only according to some intellectualized concept but in truth, so that one can grasp it with the hands. . . .

Only the person who knows Jesus to be the Conqueror who liberates us, who knows him as the Captain of our salvation leading us up out of all destruction — only he comes under the proclamation of salvation in a truly humble spirit. . . . When, for example, an habitual liar is attracted to the gospel, when the truth dawns that he is being saved and he believes it, what about his lying now? Shall he let his lies continue because he believes? What is the dynamic behind his lying? Behind his lying is the power of hell that binds him to the sin. And if no change takes place and the lying retains its hold, do you suppose such a person is being saved or redeemed?

If a redemption does not break into our lives through the power of God in Jesus Christ, then, although we call ourselves Christian and even consider ourselves among the believers, we will not enter heaven. No, the cords of sin, death, and hell must be cut off. We must become new; something that originates essentially in the power of Christ must set our life upon a new course. In short, we must have *Jesus*, the Conquering One, in small as well as in great matters. Only in this way will the assured hope of eternal life become firm within us. . . .

We come now to a final proclamation which lies in the name Jesus. If we lay hold upon Jesus as the Redeemer of our own lives, then we can also believe him to be the power of God leading the life of all creation to the light. The *power* of Jesus Christ, too, we can relate to the whole of mankind, just as the *understanding* of salvation has been related to the entire world. When I know Jesus, who he is and what divine powers are manifested in him, then I have courage not only for myself but for others as well.

Even though many people nowadays accept nothing of their own salvation because they understand nothing of it, I am not discouraged by this. I think to myself, "Just wait until you have been rescued out of the claws of death, until your eyes have been opened; then you will believe!" It is such an attitude, I am convinced, which the name Jesus must create in the hearts of believers. Then these believers will become the firstfruits, the light and salt, the front-line fighters in behalf of others. And herein lies the significance of the church of Christ on earth, the body of Christ which is to fill all things with its glory. . . .

The life of man can no longer be an idle tale, since Jesus lives. Rather, the life of man is to come under the power of eternal life; and the Savior wants to help us in this. Indeed, as the great Lord of heaven and earth, he wants to fight at our side. For the world's sake, he wants us to lay hold of him who is the power of God on earth. It is this power that blesses what is cursed, that rescues what is lost, and that finally wins the victory against all powers that are in heaven and that carry their anti-God activity down as far as hell.

This Jesus we have come to know; this Jesus we preach; this Jesus we want to take with us through each day of the year. And though one generation after another apostatize, one society after another be destroyed, let them fall away, let them go where they will! *You* lay hold on Jesus!

With him, we hold the victory in our hands; with him we will yet bring the world back in. Even if the whole world should mock him, if only our little flock remains steadfast in hoping for his power, we will yet see the whole world become our reward.

The whole of creation must come under the church of Jesus Christ, who is the head of all things. This purpose cannot fail; its expression is the word of God, the Father's child given to us as Jesus—and such a word of God cannot fail. . . .

The name Jesus will not find its glory in his allowing mankind to sink to ruin, in billions dying away in hell. Rather, the glory of that name will come in his being surrounded by countless multitudes, all, all of whom he has wrested from the power of death and sin, so that not one can say that he was saved apart from the right hand of God, the Father's might who is named Jesus.

ALL THINGS NEW

> And I heard a great voice from the throne saying, "Behold, the dwelling of God is with men. He will dwell with them, and they shall be his people, and God himself will be with them; he will wipe away every tear from their eyes, and death shall be no more, neither shall there be mourning nor crying nor pain any more, for the former things have passed away." And he who sat upon the throne said, "Behold, I make all things new." Also he said, "Write this, for these words are trustworthy and true." And he said to me, "It is done! I am the Alpha and the Omega, the beginning and the end. To the thirsty I will give water without price from the fountain of the water of life. He who conquers shall have this heritage, and I will be his God and he shall be my son."
>
> (Rev. 21:3 – 7)

These words express the warmest, most intimate possible relationship to the will of God. And this will of God has become so deeply rooted in mankind through Jesus Christ that it can never again be disregarded. And although the whole of human society temporarily should be unmindful of it, and though Christendom itself should be moving on a track very different from that which this will of God prescribes, there always will arise out of this root which has penetrated humanity people who will be as intimately bound up with the will of God as were the apostles and the prophets. These are people who will know that everything else derives from this unswerving, relentless will of God to make all things new — everything both for our own personal lives with all their woes and obstacles, storms and defeats, and also for a human race which has been forced to pass through so much trouble, so many defeats, and so many disappointments.

In Christ people can know and experience that we stand in an on-going process, a progressive development, that is leading to a consummation, to an end of which it will be said: "Behold, the dwelling of God is with men; behold, all things become new." All sorrow will have ceased, even the blackness of death. The death of man will have been transcended through a creative act of God, so that the struggles in which we still stand today will have come to their end.

The Lord Jesus, so to speak, always stands at the far borders of the present. Consequently, it is understandable that, for him and for his first disciples, it seemed that at one blow things could all be different tomorrow. We may think that they were deluded; but if so, it was a glorious delusion and the greatest of truths. If Jesus had hesitated to step out to the remotest boundary and say, "The present may come to an end tomorrow," then he would not have been that powerful personality who again and again calls into being people who, in view of present things approaching their end, derive strength to overcome that which still needs to be overcome today. We want to be such people; we would step out to the border, too. A part of our being has terminated its dealings with the present; we stand out there at the border, at the boundary of the present world, the boundary which signifies the beginning of a new humanity.

To be sure, it did not happen when the apostles expected it to — and their expectations may have been rather crass — as though all things could change overnight, as though all the evils in the world could be removed in one fell swoop. The day, of course, has lengthened; and now we know that the first day which Jesus introduced involves an extended period of development. The day is in the process of becoming; it is not completed.

But what are a thousand years in the development of mankind? What are two thousand years? As we think of it today, what are the two thousand years that lie behind us? What is time? We need not be concerned about the length of time, if only we are involved in the cause, if only we are standing where we ourselves can grow in the will of God along with this larger development. And when the consummation does take place, when all things will have been fulfilled, then we will look back on what seems a brief span of years and say, rejoicing, "It has indeed come quickly."

Therefore, I would like to direct a request to all of us: "Let us take our stand at the end of things." That is a loaded request. When we stand at the border, we already begin to experience many things in a different way. We discover that the incurable illness in us and about us actually comes to an end; a new thing begins. When we focus on the time to come, as Jesus does, then we already have drawn something of the time to come into our present life.

This age of tedium, emptiness, and restlessness which torments us cannot conquer us. Those evils which find expression in sorrow and crying and death and darkness, they will discover in us a power which will overcome them. This is what our scripture means by "he who conquers"; we who stand in this will of God for the age to come already conquer indescribably much now, even though we do not play leading roles. We cannot proudly say, "I will conquer, don't worry; nothing can harm me. With my faith I can get through." Although we personally do and should feel ourselves to be weak and poor, it is something of the power of the Lord Jesus that does the conquering, a power that can overcome all things because it is the power of God.

This power overcomes everything evil in us already in this present time, to the point that we cannot even say that anything is proving truly difficult for us. And even though we may be confronted by something extremely disagreeable, even if we are forced to renounce all we have come to love, we will still retain the consciousness that the power of God will overcome the difficult in us; we will not be destroyed by the pitiful stuff that surrounds us. . . .

"I make all things new!" This was the main source of power

113

for Jesus as long as he was on earth. This is the source of power and might which arises in man again and again through the Spirit of Christ, so that he may not keep on working foolishly with externals but may be inspired to hope that all things will indeed become new. What to us is the world with all its evils if we have become strong in the Spirit of God? Who can name anything that could make us afraid if we are strong in the Spirit of God? When we have become new, then we conquer all things.

IN THE RETURN OF JESUS CHRIST

And he told them a parable, to the effect that they ought always to pray and not lose heart. He said, "In a certain city there was a judge who neither feared God nor regarded man; and there was a widow in that city who kept coming to him and saying, 'Vindicate me against my adversary.' For a while he refused; but afterward he said to himself, 'Though I neither fear God nor regard man, yet because this widow bothers me, I will vindicate her, or she will wear me out by her continual coming.' " And the Lord said, "Hear what the unrighteous judge says. And will not God vindicate his elect, who cry to him day and night? Will he delay long over them? I tell you, he will vindicate them speedily. Nevertheless, when the Son of man comes, will he find faith on earth?"   (Luke 18:1 – 8)

In this parable on prayer there is something of a history of the coming of Jesus Christ. Today all our life of faith in the Savior, all our praying, even as individuals, all we do and experience — everything takes place under the portent of the return of the Lord Jesus.

The Savior comes into a dreadful world; although he is the Coming One, the world into which he comes is one of terrible unrighteousness. This is the characteristic of world history. World history always crushes a great number — an infinitely great number — of people under its brutal, violent tread. The history of the world may take what course it will — even in the eras of greatness for some nations, in the zenith of their culture, as they say — one thing cannot change, do what you like: history tramples people to the earth; behind it rises the cry of the destitute and the poor, whom the world is utterly unable to help. All worldly wisdom is confounded; it has nothing of value to offer. Even the good which is attempted leads to unrighteousness again and leaves behind it a moraine, an evil track in which lies the rubble of broken bones. And it is into *this* city that the Savior comes. . . .

But because the Savior has come, we do not see only here and there a widow or a destitute person given a bit of help by the unrighteous judge, the civic authority. No, we see much help streaming forth from the coming of Jesus Christ. Then we rejoice; yes, then we rejoice. The return of Jesus Christ, our Savior, is truly happening within the world — even though it now is known only quietly in a few individuals, the elect. The Savior looks to his elect within this sorry world. And perhaps with a bit of anxiety — as the last line of our text indicates — he clings, as it were, to these elect ones, seeking a base, a beachhead, for his coming. . . .

He is looking about among us, too, and is asking: "Are any of the elect here? Is there someone here who takes delight in the history which God is effecting on earth for the sake of his kingdom, for the redemption which is coming to pass?" And if you, dear child, have a love for the coming Savior, and if your heart persistently says, "Lord Jesus, *our* cause is nothing; Lord Jesus, come! Yea, come, Lord Jesus," then the Savior says to you: "Pray without ceasing! Do not let up! Do not become foolish, and do not be without understanding! Pray!"

Through prayer we must set ourselves into the return of Jesus Christ, into the history of his coming to the world. And I give you the advice, I would almost say the command: If you pray regarding any matter, even concerning material needs, then place yourselves within the coming of the Savior. . . .

And even when we individually experience help (and I receive so much help that often I am embarrassed in the presence of other people), then we must always ask uneasily: "Does this come from the return of my Lord Jesus Christ?" And if it does come from this return, then it is a sign that the Savior *is* coming. Then I shout for joy; then I rejoice; then I am exultant; then I am comforted! A sign of the coming Savior! I do not know what else can give me joy on earth. *Today* there is something of the return of Jesus Christ. . . .

How is it today? Does *our* praying stand fully under this portent? Does the Savior here and now have people who believe in him as the Coming One, so that he can find a base of operations on earth? There certainly is much praying: you pray; your neighbor prays; your enemy prays; your adversary prays; everybody prays. But you pray in your sin, in your pride, in your passion. You pray, and the world remains as it was. The adversary laughs us to scorn for our praying. He is kept from laughing only if we stand within the return of Jesus Christ! "When the Son of man comes, will he find faith on earth?" No, he will not find faith unless we pray within the coming of the kingdom of God in the person of the Lord Jesus. . . .

Granted, the world does not believe all this; but the Savior *is* coming in any case. Granted, too, the elect no longer believe; but the Savior *is* coming even so. And perhaps even the elect, by and large, must fall into a form of unbelief so that the word, the great word, can be fulfilled: "For God has consigned all men to disobedience, that he may have mercy upon all."

But what then, Christendom, have you to claim in superiority over the pagans? Of what is it you want to boast against the unbelievers? How dare you insult others when in the main point, the point about which the Lord Jesus is primarily concerned, you also are lacking, when you are not standing in the return of God in Jesus Christ, when you are not standing firm in this coming?

For ourselves, we renounce everything — all being pious, all acting as though we were holy upon earth, all boasting. We forget all this, and as little children we slip in under the cloak of the great and mighty Lord and Savior, Jesus Christ. He is coming; and even if you do not believe, redemption from the adversary will finally break into your own personal life. The Lord Jesus will come despite all unbelief! May he help us; may God help us that we might pray in the coming of Jesus Christ!

WAIT FOR THE LORD

Our soul waits for the Lord; he is our help and shield.

(Psa. 33:20)

W*e want to be those who in truth wait for the Lord. But for* what purpose do we wait? Do you suppose that our waiting is simply a kind of religiosity, by virtue of which we are perhaps differently tuned religiously than other Christians? Is this to be only a particular religious coloring that signifies nothing further?

Such may be the attitude of some who say they wait for the Lord, but in whose lives nothing is changed in consequence. Our waiting for the Lord is to lead to *deeds* of the Lord; consequently, our opinion is: If I wait for the Lord, the Lord will soon come.

We cannot understand those who say, "I wait for the Lord, but it will be a long time before he comes." If a person says this and believes it, why does he wait at all? He had better leave it be altogether. This I say: He who does not in all things expect God *soon* is not waiting. Even if he affirms ten thousand times that he is waiting for the Lord, I do not believe it. If, for example, you come into severe illness, and in it you wait for the Lord, can you postpone the expectation of his answer twenty or thirty years or even longer? Impossible! If it is to be real waiting, you must expect God to do something at once. In consequence, perhaps tomorrow even will bring his decisive help.

For the person who waits for the Lord, everything he awaits in hope already comes into view. I think of this waiting as something alive in me; and obviously that which is alive is sustained with food. What, then, is the bread of waiting? The bread of waiting is the deeds of God. Without the deeds of God, the waiting of the heart dies.

Yet we must not expect too much from our hearts alone. Surely we do not consider ourselves strong enough that we can say, "I *wait* for the Lord, but for the time being I don't *need* him. I'll manage somehow." Yes, you will manage all right; but how? In an ungodly way, just as the world manages, where God is permitted to be nothing but a spectator. It ought not to be so. Rather, when I wait, my waiting should be grounded in the acts of the Lord. My waiting acquires its durability because the Lord performs his actions. And my waiting will find its goal in a great action of God performed upon me and upon all creation.

We have experienced that the Lord is our help and shield, and that is why we *can* wait. Also, we have experienced that the Lord can become our help and shield suddenly, surprisingly. Thus, we always wait for the Lord in such a way as to expect an early manifestation from him; we cannot imagine that there will be boredom when dealing with the Lord.

"He is our help," that is, he snatches us out of the evils into which we have come — body, soul, and spirit. It is not necessary, of course, that there be impressive, outwardly visible miracles. If only in the secret places, quietly, things are set right again and we are not left tangled in evil, then we are helped. Those who wait for the Lord already see his help, while others see only misfortune and ruin. Those who wait notice that the Lord sets to work immediately to remove the evil; and thus they are assured of near and complete salvation.

How easy it is then to remain patient, even when burden and threat persist. But it is unbearable when one is caught in some evil and then must admit, "The Savior is not at work here." Of course, I know very well that there are many people in the world who see in themselves and in others the most unhappy of conditions. These people put up with the worst sort of evil in themselves with the evasion, "That's simply the way I am." It does not matter to them whether the Savior sets to work with them or not. And they view the misery of the world the same way. It is a matter of perfect indifference to them whether or not the Savior puts his hand to the problem. They may be a little sorry that things are the way they are, but even that does not trouble them for long.

But the person who waits for the Lord cannot feel this way; he wants to see God's action everywhere. When there is something amiss or distorted, something sinful or pitiful in the world, he wishes day and night that God might set to work. He prays that God will remember his name, "merciful and gracious, slow to anger, and abounding in steadfast love and faithfulness" (Exod. 34:6).

And then God puts his hand to the task; he is ready to grasp the whole world and, through Jesus Christ, switch it onto another track, pleasing to himself. It is those who wait who know how much in earnest God is about this; and they see, already in our time, how much has taken place. If we wait for the Lord, we are not waiting to see the *beginning* of our redemption. If those who believe that the consummation of the kingdom of God has been postponed indefinitely would consider how much God has been at work until now, they would be surprised. Truly, we are no longer waiting for the beginning; we are waiting for *the end*. We stand in the midst of the acts of God which are purposed for the end.

If anyone ridicules us because we wait for the Lord, expecting the end to come soon, it is simply because he does not know what waiting people experience. Those who wait for the Lord experience so much of the intervention of God that they have no time to make calculations for the distant future. Today, tomorrow, and always, they are in a state of readiness for the experience of new things; and each day they are prepared for the greatest event of all, the coming of the Lord. . . .

But the Lord is also our shield. Innumerable dangers come upon the one who waits, particularly when he is moving forward. The last times, judged outwardly, are the most evil of times. This will be our own experience as well. Yet, in this, God also permits us the daily experience that we are protected children. Often we can see this only in retrospect. When suddenly some terrible evil breaks in on us, frightening and scattering all the people, we are tempted to think, "How can God permit such a thing?" But soon we come to realize that, in the midst of the greatest danger, we have experienced the greatest protection. God was showing us in what great danger we stand, how everything in the world is set toward destruction, and how much on guard we must be.

If things were otherwise, we would become too secure. If we were not subject to these sudden storms (which are, of course, only a small fraction of the distress in which the world lies), who knows but that we might become lax in our waiting? But to those who wait for the Lord, God is a shield. We can experience this; and it is an encouragement for the remainder of the time of our waiting. . . .

Yet how few wait on the Lord in this way! Many Christians are surprised when they hear of some extraordinary thing happening to those who wait for the Lord! *They* wait and expect nothing; they believe but anticipate no change; and because nothing happens with them, they don't believe it happens with others either. But all of you who even now have found the Lord to be a help and a shield, you can learn of such things more and more!

However, if I wait for the Lord, I also wait on behalf of the whole world to which I belong. The Chinese are as much on my heart as is my own person. Yet here we are waiting, and others are not waiting with us, and that is hard. Yet ultimately those who wait for the Lord must succeed. Suddenly it will become bright over the whole earth — to the praise of God and of our Savior, Jesus Christ. May he send joyful hope and victorious confidence into our hearts even in the darkest days so we may wait through to the end and be saved at last.

Lo, I am with you always, to the close of the age. (Matt. 28:20)

The Savior's being with us has reference to the end of the world, not to its continuance. All the days of the disciples of Jesus are workdays looking forward to the consummation of the kingdom of God, with which event the present futile world will come to an end.

In the special sense of our text, Jesus is not *with* a person who spends his days for the sole purpose of sustaining earthly life. The Lord does not wish to spend too much effort on the continuance of the world. After all, it is corruptible; there is nothing left to be done but to await the wearing out of the decaying structure and the creating of a new one.

For the time being, we must do the best we can with what we have, not being too frightened when at times things collapse under our feet. We are only being loosed from everything earthly. Never again will the disciples of Jesus be really comfortable; but in view of the end coming upon the world, we can bear that which is inconvenient. Even the last great tribulation can be borne easily in view of that end.

In all our work, then, let us be careful to fix our eyes, not on the continuance of the world, but on its end. Then the Lord will be with us always, and he will see us through our current needs as well.

STANDING BEFORE THE SON OF MAN

"And there will be signs in the sun and moon and stars, and upon the earth distress of nations in perplexity at the roaring of the sea and the waves, men fainting with fear and with foreboding of what is coming on the world; for the powers of the heavens will be shaken. And then they will see the Son of man coming in a cloud with power and great glory. Now when these things begin to take place, look up and raise your heads, because your redemption is drawing near."

And he told them a parable: "Look at the fig tree, and all the trees; as soon as they come out in leaf ... the summer is already near. So also, when you see these things taking place, you know that the kingdom of God is near." (Luke 21:25 – 31)

Nothing is more important than that we prepare ourselves to stand before the Son of Man. In answer to the question, "What should be a person's prime concern in this life?" we say: that he have a sure hope of eternal life. Yet we interpret that answer to mean that, in this life, he have an attitude enabling him to stand before the Son of Man. . . .

There is a question that strikes fear into our hearts; and every honest person will feel with me. It is this: Will I be able to stand before God? Will I be able to stand before the Savior? Many people who feel quite reassured because they attend church every Sunday and participate in religious activities — who may even be reckoned among the most devout — would nevertheless be terrified if suddenly they should hear the thunder of the last judgment and witness the arrival of our God. They would then come to see their Christian cloak as a filthy garment. In order to stand before God, they would be forced to look to something very different from what they could muster in the way of piety and spirituality, even in the best sense of those words.

But, beloved, we should not let ourselves come to this terror. We who are disciples of Jesus are to take care of that terror beforehand. It is our responsibility to consider ourselves always as standing before the Son of Man, to examine ourselves as though now, in the next hour, heaven would open and the time of the end come. This should be our attitude; and in such an attitude we can experience in advance something of the appearance of Jesus Christ and the coming of God into the world. . . .

In the midst of earthly existence, we are surrounded by the heavenly and the eternal, that which gives movement and life to our hearts and sets us, as it were, already halfway into heaven. While we carry on our earthly activities quite naturally and normally, our hearts can still be in the heavenly and have experiences there where our eternal home is. Such a time we would very much like to experience. We would particularly like to have it now as we observe Christendom deteriorating and becoming bound up in the temporal. . . .

All we have had up to this point is on its last run downwards. Our theology is moving down with the rapidity of a lowering storm. Our ecclesiastical perceptions are rapidly becoming political perceptions. Our worship services are being accommodated to the world. And thus it is necessary that all that has been should cease, should come to its end, making room again for something new, namely, the kingdom of God.

And we have a certain right to expect this in our time. At least I would like to stand before you as a witness of the truth that we are living in a day when we can expect the end of that which has been and can hope for the new. . . . Together with those who belong to me and all those who wish to understand me, my one aim shall be to permit that which has been to die, to cease. Of course, this is to take place in spirit, not outwardly. God wants to introduce some new thing; and the Savior will be better able to live in us when we ourselves no longer want to amount to so much — when we acknowledge that in what has been until now there is much that is detrimental, much that is of the flesh, much *human* activity, although the intentions were good.

All of this must die; therefore, we now say: "Die, then *Jesus* will live." As up to this point we have said, "Jesus is victor against the devil, against hell, and against death," we now leave it all off to one side and say: "Enough of that; now another conflict must begin: Jesus is victor against *the flesh.*" So you may no longer expect me to grapple with the devil; it is no longer necessary, and I shall leave him aside. . . .

It is more important that the Savior overcome *us* than that he continue to attack the devil. The devil is not so significant; we ourselves are much more truly the opposition to the kingdom of God. We who are in the flesh offer much more resistance to the kingdom of God than the devil does. Human self-will, earthly-mindedness, and greed; the will to power and the love of fame; human heroism which does not need God but in the strength of youth accomplishes what it chooses without consulting God — these overleap the commandments of God and prove more dangerous than the devil. If in our day we wish to fight as we ought, then we must turn against these foes.

You will understand, of course, that in this conflict one does not advance *heroically*, as one does in fighting the devil. Here one becomes weak. And here I need to become the weakest among you. Only in dying do I want to become the strongest among you — in self-accusation, in gladly taking the guilt of others upon myself, in willingly suffering in myself all the pain and the cares of others. In this, I want to be the strongest among you. But, beloved, I do not wish to do it alone. . . . Follow me into this much more difficult struggle in which we turn the sword upon ourselves. . . . We want to be those who are dying, because we know that very soon we must give account to the Lord for everything we have done. . . .

Our joy shall be in God alone; his honor alone we wish to

seek. Indeed, we shall willingly be those who bear burdens, who suffer, who are feeble, if only through this we can serve God the Father, Son, and Holy Spirit. Our heart burns regarding the misery of the world, because, although God has given so much help, he has received very little more honor than if he had not helped at all. People have honored him very little more because of his wonders and signs, even though these have become so great that they are spoken of everywhere. Wherever you go in the world you can hear people talking about them; but God is not honored more now because of them than he was before he performed them. . . . Consequently, our heart burns for God's honor, not for our flesh; for God's health, not for our health; for the welfare of Christ in his church, not for our earthly well-being; for the experiences of the Holy Spirit, not for the coziness of our Christian spirit. . . .

We need to die to our own *cause* as well. There is to be no "Boll Christianity"; God preserve us from that! Insofar as such already has come to be, I declare it, too, to be flesh — and flesh is of no value. Indeed, it is precisely to the flesh that we want to die; we want to be nothing special. No Christian pride is to emerge, but rather a Christian nothingness. We want to become nothing. We as Christians do not amount to anything; only Jesus does. What greatness we have achieved to this point, and what prominence we have attained beyond others, may God take from us. . . .

The times of the end are upon us. Our text says: "When these things begin to take place, look up and raise your heads, because your redemption is drawing near." And later it says: "Truly, I say to you, this generation will not pass away till all has taken place."

While, on the one hand, we are encouraged to die, we are exhorted, on the other hand, to raise our heads, because the end is already drawing near. Already the signs are noticeable in sun, moon, and stars. Already, although quietly and unobtrusively, the anxious fear of men and the collapse of human power is beginning. Already the powers of the heavens are trembling, and the coming of the Son of Man is being revealed in the clouds with great power and glory.

Of course, you are free to follow or not to follow me in this matter, but I owe it to you to say that, in recent times, the progress has been much more rapid than you perhaps suspect. I stand in the greatest expectation of things to come. Not to me only but to others as well, many signs are being revealed. ...

No one considers that God, too, should be in a position to do something occasionally; natural science so long since has come to understand everything! And yet science *knows* nothing, because in these matters it can *explain* nothing. Therefore, take note: no signs will ever be given except such as also have a natural appearance. The coming of the Savior in the clouds, even when it is visible, will be explained as a natural phenomenon. These signs, even when they are very near at hand, will not be revealed to the world as readily recognizable to everyone. Only when the trumpet sounds (which *will* be audible in the world) and quite extraordinary voices are heard, will men become aware; and then they will say: "Alas, why did we not pay attention earlier? We could have taken notice. The times have been changing. Human structures and national histories have altered. Things move so rapidly that one is hardly able to follow events. And now we finally recognize that, truly, God has done this. If we had only paid attention earlier!" That is how it will be, beloved!

Yet, by that time, the terrors of the end will have set in; only those who prepared themselves earlier will remain without fear. However, it is of great significance — even for those who enter into the terrors — that there exists a people which is not terrified; a people to whom the Savior can come quietly; people, although they are scattered over the world, through whom the Savior can open a door by which even the terrified nations can enter in, so far as they repent.

Believe it, friends, that "summer" is coming for everyone, not just for you. When these things take place, then great terror must come upon the whole earth, otherwise everything would continue in the self-same course. But, through the terror, the blossoming of the earth will occur, so that the world may take on a new character, tending toward summer, and so bear fruit for God the Creator. Thus the coming of the Savior unto those circles where his coming is expected will be the beginning of the redemption of the world, the beginning of the salvation of a new people who will at that time repent in the last judgment. Ultimately, the purpose of Zion on earth is that all nations might enter into it.

Dear friends, accept this quite simply and as children, for many misconceptions regarding the last times are in circulation — and these can keep you from regarding the time as being near. It is precisely in Christian circles that there is much error regarding expectations of the end. Some people wait for the conversion of the Jews. By the time that takes place, the end will have long since come! Some wait for the Antichrist. When that occurs, God will long since have come. You need not fear the Antichrist; you don't have to stand before *him*; you must stand before *God*, and he may come sooner than you think. All these secondary matters, produced by human thinking, become obstructions for many Christians — to the point that they never honor God, never honor Christ, never honor the Holy Spirit.

Therefore, do not ponder so long upon these things; accept them simply as the Savior uttered them — because all will transpire differently from what we imagine. Those only are wise who prepare themselves to stand before the Son of Man. All other matters will take care of themselves; nothing can harm us. All the storms and all the devils may approach us — even the Antichrist may come as often as he will — nothing can harm us if we are in the Savior, if we are a Zion of God, if we have hearts that are capable of experience, if Christ lives in our hearts.

Antichrist cannot subdue Christ; and he cannot subdue me either, if Christ lives in me. But if Christ is not living in me, then, although I may be the cleverest theologian or the greatest of Christians, every fool can throw me; it wouldn't take an Antichrist to accomplish that. Therefore, beloved, what is important is that we be able to stand before God. It is about this we must concern ourselves; it is for this we must hope. . . . We should be able to observe how the day of the Lord makes its approach. The text says that, in observing it, it is as though you were to see summer coming. Just as, in the gardens and fields, one can observe the first blossoms opening, the trees beginning to bud, and the leaves emerging, so we are to be a people that experiences the summer of God — the rising of the Father, the light of the Savior, the radiance of the Holy Spirit, the glory of the Sabbath of God.

All this we are to experience; but we will have to be quiet so that the Savior can show it to us. There are plenty of inquisitive people who would like to know something very special; but God does not tell them anything. When we experience something, we must remain perfectly quiet and make no great commotion about it; we must not storm and shout and seek to convert everybody to it. Just let it all come into your heart!

God does not reveal anything to a person who will immediately shout it abroad. But if we become sensible and rate the kingdom of God higher than anything else, then a kingdom-year can come and we will experience it. Yet we must pray for it, too, standing before God quietly and unitedly; then it will come.

In the meantime, the signs are occurring, although much depends on our becoming persons who can sense the approach of summer. God can join himself to such people; they are utterly free from all that is in the world. You may be rich or poor, glad or sad; you may be in any situation you like; it is all secondary. Those who can observe and who are able to experience what they observe — they stand above the world. Of course, they live in the world and do business in the world; but the joy of their hearts is the experiences of the kingdom which are theirs.

God is near, and the Spirit of God is near, and already the signs are present in which we can recognize the end. People may believe it or not; but the word must be said; and the Lord makes his word come true.

GOD SO LOVED THE WORLD

For God so loved the world that he gave his only Son, that whoever believes in him should not perish but have eternal life. For God sent the Son into the world, not to condemn the world, but that the world might be saved through him. He who believes in him is not condemned; he who does not believe is condemned already, because he has not believed in the name of the only Son of God. And this is the judgment, that the light has come into the world, and men loved darkness rather than light, because their deeds were evil. For every one who does evil hates the light, and does not come to the light, lest his deeds should be exposed. But he who does what is true comes to the light, that it may be clearly seen that his deeds have been wrought in God.
(John 3:16 – 21)

Actually, *it is impossible to preach on this text; one can only repeat* it. It is already as complete as possible a sermon upon what God is in the world, what he was, and what he will be in the world forever.

We human beings usually see only our own neighborhood, the area in which we live; and what we see there is *darkness*. Thus the perspectives of God are lost, and everything seems beyond help. It looks as though all is lost. And then a great sadness comes over people; they see only themselves. The sadness becomes indifference, the indifference turns to insolence, and out of insolence grows thoughtlessness. And thus we move farther and farther from God. Finally, the mass of humanity despairs of God, is hardly capable of thinking of him at all; they do not know anymore who God is. Despite all their best efforts, this humanity does not achieve a satisfying existence. One can offer them what one will, lay treasure and fortune at their feet; they devour them and remain as they were. That is the darkness.

Do not imagine that people in darkness can be helped through any earthly treasure or fortune. One can only intoxicate them with money and excite them with innovations. There is tremendous activity and struggle for life in the darkness. There always appears to be progress; yet, things always remain as they were. Finally, all the aspirations of people and all their works die again; it all turns into a heap of rubble. What is left of all the Egyptians who wished to eternalize themselves even in death? What is left of all the ancient nations that had such a tremendous life in the darkness? There is nothing but ruin.

Yet into this darkness in which men perceive the world from their own perspective and in which they carry on their affairs, God sends his Son and suddenly introduces a very different light, a different way of looking at things. We give up everything as lost; he simply gives up nothing as lost. God loves the world; and the world is his. Just because we have run around in the world foolishly for a time, that does not mean the world is lost.

What then is the world? We are *in* the world; but *we* are not the world. The world is the creation of God, full of life. In this creation of God all things live — even the stones are alive. Nothing is dead, everything grows, everything develops; and in everything there is the power of life derived from God, a power demonstrating itself in a million ways, unseen and yet perceptible. A great portion of mankind is sighing; indeed, the whole world in which we live sighs for God, has its life only from God — and we are part and parcel of this world.

And now God sends his Son into the world as a man, so that mankind might recognize his love for the world and might love the world, too. In particular, we are to love the world as God's creation, not the world which the apostle speaks of when he says, "Do not love the world," the world of sin. But what God created is loved by God; and it certainly is not given up merely because people become foolish and can no longer help themselves in the darkness.

God does not give up on the people, either — indeed, on the people least of all. They are to be the children of the Father in heaven; and, as the first among the living creatures, they are to mediate the light of God to the world, for the world is wretched as long as man is not prepared to carry the light of God into it.

Therefore, in the beginning, when man still belonged to God, there was *paradise*. When man was no longer God's, paradise ceased. When Jesus, the Son of God, came into the world, there was paradise again. His coming constituted a new beginning; people drew life from the Creator again. In a very simple way, therefore, people who encountered Jesus could be filled with blessedness; they were revived inwardly and outwardly. He had words of life, so they were in paradise; for, where words of life are heard again, there *is* paradise. The world that is loved of God is our heaven — if we understand the love of God and receive it into ourselves.

Therefore, the first truth is this: The world, as God's world, is not hated by Jesus, nor is it discarded or condemned or cursed by him. No; precisely as the man under commission by God, he must *love* the world — because God loved the world. When God sent his Son, he gave him the charge: "Love my beloved world, no matter what you may experience, even if you are crucified. It is not the world that does this to you but the poor people who do not understand. Therefore, do not be misled; love my beloved world! I created it; I am the Father of all that lives in it, and this fatherhood I will not surrender. Every living creature, everything that has breath, is mine; I have enclosed all these things in my heart, and there they will remain. Go, love the world; do not judge it. How it came to be in darkness is none of your business. You are my Son; be my Son, the Son of the Father who loves the world!"

Thus, the light has arisen, and we are to enter this light; then we will be filled with life together with the Son. Consequently, the world suddenly becomes good. To believe in the Son means nothing other than giving up the evil which has engulfed us until now and whose adherents we have become. It means coming to the place where God is with his love, where Jesus is, the Son who is bearer and executor of nothing other than the love of God with which he loves the world.

Arise, then; be radiant and joyful; believe in his name; and then you are in the light and are saved. For this purpose the Son of God becomes mighty in the love of God toward you as soon as you open your ears and say: "Praise and thanks be to God! God loves the world; now I too want to be filled with love toward all that lives. If Jesus, his Son, is only love, then I want to be only love as well. I am enabled to become a follower of this Son; therefore, together with him, I belong to God; I am loved and I love. And where love is, there is life; and where life is, there is the light of men."

In this way men are to come out from *judgment*. Before this, they are under judgment; now one need not judge them, because they already are unhappy and feel rejected. One need not add to that. Oh, dear friends, do not make any person more evil than he is! There has been enough of judgment. Some day it will become evident to what extent many disciples of Jesus have hurt the world, which already could have become aware that the love of God has come. But no, we feel we have to wait until people become sensible. People who already believe in Jesus throw one stone after another upon the poor world! In doing so, they ultimately condemn themselves again; and then they themselves cease to believe in the love of God—and thus the darkness has become thicker than it was before!

Therefore, we must begin anew; we must understand the love of God anew. But don't waste time pondering it! Become children and accept it for what is is. Permit this love which has never yet been fully understood, permit this love with which God has loved the world, to dwell with you as the Holy Spirit. This *is* the Holy Spirit—the love of God for the world. This love is what flows from the Holy Spirit, this and nothing else. Do not believe that anything condemnatory is the Holy Spirit of God. God's Spirit is love. It is the same Spirit that spoke in the midst of the darkness, "Let there be light!" Sin was there, too. It is the same Spirit that said, "Let the darkness be separated from the light!" and the world became new.

In the same way, the world as it is now will become new in Jesus Christ. Nothing else need take place except that the love of God penetrate into all things. The hatred which has entered into man must finally be eradicated. Believe in Jesus Christ, and do not hate! To believe in him means to love; and, in so doing, you are relatives and friends of the only begotten Son. When you are rooted in him, all melancholy is a thing of the past. All sin is removed, because through the love of God one has entered upon a new way, one has become a totally new person. What concern now is that dead past?

Whoever does not experience this remains in misery. Many try in their wretchedness to create some kind of religion to assure their happiness after death. Be happy in love right now, from this day forward. Begin to love! Love one another! Boll would become a paradise in one year's time if everyone here had this love of God in his heart. This needs to be grasped. Receive the full love of God, and you will be separated from your sins. There is no longer anything that condemns, because you yourselves have left the old, have become new persons, new creatures. All things have become new!

We need not wait for some special event; there is enough of blessedness now, because the love of God is effective in creating blessedness. Much creative work takes place now, because the living word is present, reviving the person both inwardly and outwardly. Suddenly someone says, "I was dead and have become alive again!" A sick person says, "I have become perfectly happy; I don't know where my sickness went to!" One lying at the point of death breathes again and does not die; an insane person is cured.

Oh, you have no inkling how many creative works take place simply because of this love of God! People are planted upon new foundations for living, foundations which have been present all along, though unused. Everything necessary is present already; but it becomes effective only where Jesus is and where one understands the love of God in Jesus. There, all things come to life; and the more people come to understand this love, the better. Indeed, even animals and plants will become new when finally people come to understand this love.

My friends, this is the signal which God has given the world. Until today it has not been understood, and that is what required such long development. This is the judgment, that in the face of the love of God the terrible misery and woe of mankind really comes to the surface. Through the Jesus who came to save sinners, all blessedness and all life have been laid at the feet of humanity. And now people run away. This is the judgment, this is the misery, that people love their present situation more than the light, because they are afraid that their present evil will become manifest.

You have no idea what a terrible hindrance this is, this which keeps sinners from exposing themselves. If only I could say to all of the very worst of people, "Surrender what you are concealing; do not be afraid!" Their works have been evil; and now they are afraid to come to the light, because they fear that Jesus will condemn them all the more severely. So they run away from the light.

No; out with that which is hidden! Out with the evil you have done! To the light with it! The light will not harm you; do not be afraid of the Father in heaven! Do not suppose that you will be saved because you say, "I have been good." Our sins must be submitted to the love of God; we must become exposed for what we are. It is to this love that we reveal ourselves; and the love separates us from our sins.

Many people are robbed of their peace, because they are

afraid that others will not like them anymore if all the evil comes out. But God likes you anyway, even if no human being does. People, of course, do get insulting when another person lets it all come out. Almost everybody steals and lies, but woe to the one in whom it is exposed! Everyone rails at him. But God does not behave in that way; he likes you anyway.

Our attitude toward people must change, my friends, or we will never experience the kingdom of God. With such hating and judging we frighten the noblest sinners away from the gates of the kingdom of God. Yes, there are actually the noblest of people among the sinners. Many a person is buried in the mud of sin and is yet the most brilliant gem. But God so loved that each person now may have the courage to say: "I am going to the Savior, too. I will take my lying to the Savior, and then I will become a new person. I *want* to become exposed so that all that is evil can be brought to the light. And there I will be loved; I will not be condemned."

You must proclaim it; say it to yourselves and to others: "God will not condemn us! Come, let us be honest before the Father in heaven. Let us go to Jesus, to the one man who can love us. Let us become a church that has nothing but love!" Yes, we can bring things to this very point; even the evil we have done will be seen in a new light, in our understanding of the God who says: "Be at peace, my child. Even the evil that occurred was under my control. There is no thought now of your earlier presence among the pigs. My son was dead, and has come to life again."

Now all is love, peace, and joy in the Holy Spirit. That Spirit is the very simplest expression of what God is. Other spirits have sought to mingle with this one; and men have structured philosophies of the Spirit and supposed they were clever. Finally, they have tossed the whole gospel out of the window; so instead of the Holy Spirit they have spirits, instead of the gospel they have an almost fear-inspiring proclamation, and instead of a heart full of joy and power in the Father they have a melancholy heart. Rather than people being joyful as partakers of the love of God, they are sad. Thus the world and sin become greater and greater; and God becomes very small. Yet, in truth, our God is much greater than all sin and all the world. But his life must truly be in our hearts; and then it will become evident that Jesus Christ is the love of God.

WHO FORGIVES ALL YOUR INIQUITY

Through this man Jesus forgiveness of sins is proclaimed to you, and by him every one that believes is righteous.
(Acts 13:38 – 39; from the German.)

This is the way of it! The Savior slips into us; and when anyone else wants to enter and demand a right to us, then he has to deal with the Savior. Our natural, sinful man is put behind; and the Savior steps forward and says, "What do you want? I stand security for this man. You have no more business here."

Even if the person still has a sin, he no longer has to negotiate about it; that is now the Savior's concern. And in this respect the person *is* righteous; no accuser can begin proceedings against him. Yet *the Savior* still negotiates with us regarding our sin. We must not be so stupid, as some evangelical Christians are, as to think that even God never deals with us regarding our sins. We are not righteous in the sense that God will no longer censure that which is sin, but rather in the sense that God now has us where he wants us, where he can do something with us. Yet, surely, he cannot leave us as the tramps we are.

It is here that we make a terrible blunder; and this is the glaring misunderstanding between the Evangelical and the Catholic Churches. One is as stupid as the other. The fact of the matter is simply that God sees in us only the Savior. If the Savior can get into us, then we are righteous; *but now God's dealings with us begin.* God demands from us a total *believing*, but no less a total *effort*. And these lazy Christians who run about thinking that no one will ask whether they are doing anything or not — they will run up against it! It would be well to take to heart all the seven virtues of the Catholic Church.

It is amazing how immorally pious we can be. Yet, if a person is excessively pious without having morals, he becomes a fool. When a person has entered into grace, the first requirement is that he get set properly and then consider what is right according to the gospel, that is, that he perform *works*. I can't see why we should want to do away with works. For what purpose then do I have my faith? Surely that faith must prove itself in some way. "To believe" does not mean "to think." Believing means being; and being means becoming. If I am good, then good will be produced. But faith is produced by God; and works are produced by God; and it is thus one becomes a true person.

Prior to this, a person already is righteous, in that his sins are forgiven through Jesus — but this in itself is the equivalent of God's saying, "Give me that man; I'll manage with him all right." In this way the Savior stands up for us when, as a consequence of the preaching of the gospel, we are gripped by him, by his Spirit. This too must be correctly understood. The act of believing does not lie within our power, as if we could say, "Till now I didn't want to believe; now I want to." Hold on a minute! You will be told when you are to believe; you don't simply come to the faith when you please. Faith is a gift and cannot be taken for yourself as you choose.

Of course, there are many people running about who think they have faith. They may have the language of Canaan; but they still do not believe. Often I prefer the unbeliever; at least he is honest. Faith comes out of preaching; preaching comes out of the Spirit; and the Spirit is God's.

When the Savior comes down and gives himself as the one who liberates, who delivers us through the gospel, then man breathes this redemption-air and comes in confidence to that one through whom redemption comes. Therefore, the words, "Every one who believes in him is righteous," are not meant to imply that a certain sovereignty has been given to man so that in his sins he is able to turn either to the devil or to the Savior. Rather, this is the meaning: he whom God sets within the sphere of the Savior so that he can recover his breath within the scope of redemption, this person recognizes that the help is coming to him from the Savior and consequently turns his eyes toward *him*. And it is this person who is saved. [It is not that he spied out a Savior for himself and *chose* him but that he recognized the rescuer who was at hand.] It is as though a man were drowning and then, in seeing someone on shore, is rescued.

This is faith, to have from the Savior the actual impression that he can help. Then one is saved; that is sufficient. That which we normally call "faith" is not enough. Many "believe" and yet do not have the impression that the Savior can help. And then, when they dispute against miracles, I think: "You surely don't have much of a faith. Someday, when you are sitting in hell, you will notice how little you believed that the Savior is the mighty one."

Your faith will not carry you from the earth by one hair's breadth; but the Savior will, by his miracle-working hand. We must not give the honor to our faith; the Lord Jesus shall have the honor. When a community is based upon him, then it becomes a truly evangelical church. Praise God, we have a God who makes right those who believe in him.

TRUE REPENTANCE

He also told this parable to some who trusted in themselves that they were righteous and despised others: "Two men went up into the temple to pray, one a Pharisee and the other a tax collector. The Pharisee stood and prayed thus with himself, 'God, I thank thee that I am not like other men, extortioners, unjust, adulterers, or even like this tax collector. I fast twice a week, I give tithes of all that I get.' But the tax collector, standing far off, would not even lift up his eyes to heaven, but beat his breast, saying, 'God, be merciful to me a sinner!' I tell you, this man went down to his house justified rather than the other; for every one who exalts himself will be humbled, but he who humbles himself will be exalted." (Luke 18:9 – 14)

It is not exactly easy to preach on this text. It is, of course, a message announcing the kingdom of God which, upon becoming effective in the hearer, gives God an opening to reveal his righteousness and truth on earth. Yet there is a great danger that the hearers will take this very message of repentance out of the hands of the messenger and make of it what they choose.

Every person has a natural propensity for repentance. We thirst for it, as it were, and then seize upon it when and how we choose. Thus, that which should be our first step toward God, often becomes the means by which we are estranged from God. We practice repentance only in such a way as to justify ourselves, and thus repentance becomes arrogance.

There thus come to be two forms of arrogance on earth instead of only one. The one form of arrogance belongs to the world. As long as things are going well, the world exalts itself through its own accomplishments and claims a place alongside God. The other form shows up in devout people who have justified themselves through repentance — or suppose that they have justified themselves by worshiping God in their particular way. Thus a *religious* structure emerges which presumes to set itself up alongside God, or even against God, just as the worldly structures do. These religious forms of arrogance are the more dangerous because the sacred is involved in them. . . .

We can see clearly how both sorts of arrogance showed up in the story of the Savior, how they gave him trouble in becoming the Savior he wanted to be. There were only few — very few — who were willing to give themselves up to him. Worldly arrogance — represented by King Herod and others — as it encountered Christ, obviously could not give itself up. These people wanted to profit from the Savior: he was to be good *for them*, he was to contribute *to them*; but they didn't want to give anything to him, they did not wish to give themselves up.

Yet the other side acted no differently, the devout of the land, the Pharisees, those in whom resided the actual strength of Israel, those through whom the Bible had come to the people, those who were the guardians of morality. They wanted a prophet; but when a prophet came, they did not want to give themselves up to him. They wanted to remain what they were; and God was supposed to serve them just as they were. That is how it was in those times, and the apostles later had to struggle against the same thing in the early church. People again used repentance and faith to fabricate a religion which took the ground right out from under God's feet.

And what shall I say about how it is today? . . . In our day human society in general has attained tremendous proficiency. It creates conditions and arrangements without the need of any help from God. In trade and traffic which have been promoted by machines of all kinds, in human employment as it has been arranged and is in progress everywhere, one does not require

God. On the thoroughfare of life one needs steam engines and machines and the like; nothing else is necessary. One does not need God as a power.

This character, more than anything else, makes our age what it is. And in this age in which everything is moving forward with such human proficiency, there must at some point be a people who cry out: "Halt! Halt! It must not be like this! God be merciful to me a sinner!" Our religion, our Christianity, our church, our best arrangements, our progress in culture, our social life, all these together must teach us to cry: "God be merciful to me a sinner!" That is the opening for the kingdom of God.

It takes courage to become quiet and to contemplate these things a little, to force them out of human hands so that one can come to faith again and stand as a poor person before God, acknowledging the truth that all this splendid life is of no use regarding that which is most important. Indeed, human proficiency ultimately leads to an end which must be called "destruction" — unless new powers enter into the process, powers of God, the rule of God wherein Christ can reign and be victorious, living and bringing into being what God wills rather than what man wills.

Will we achieve this? I hope so. Therefore, I present my old slogan again and will keep saying it until somebody understands: "Die, then Jesus will live!"

Perhaps you understand a little now what I mean by dying: surrender! When you die physically you must surrender your best, your body; and that is difficult to do, is it not? Why is it you must surrender it? Because, as it now is, it cannot live. In its present condition it is destroyed; one cannot make any eternal use of it.

At some point, every person inevitably has the feeling that he cannot continue any longer. And as painful and as unnatural as the surrender of the body is, one finally longs for it. It is similar with our inner being. Therefore, when he appears among us, the Savior says, "Give me your best! In me, die to your best, because,

143

as you have it today, it serves no good purpose. You must take it out of your hand and put it into mine." . . .

Do you willingly surrender that which you have created and which is your own, so that you offer yourself completely to God as Christ offered himself to God on the cross and placed everything into God's hand? Can you surrender like that? . . .

In our day, God wants us no longer to be proud toward others; rather, we are to be humble, as was the tax collector of our scripture. We are in need of a justification before God; we do not need any sort of self-justification! All these books and sermons which praise us as world reformers do us no good. But when we stand as poor sinners and say, "Father in heaven, we have lost out; our cause is done for. Everything we have is so saturated with the human, has taken such wrong directions, even has so much blasphemy in it, that we give everything back to you. Here we stand; God be merciful to us sinners," . . . then to us the Savior must say, "It is your fault that I am being blasphemed among the people, because what you Christians have is not what I brought. You have built your church exactly as *you* wanted it." Today matters are such that God must adjust himself to every person's ideas. Whatever way a person may choose to practice his piety, God must submit to it. In each church he must don a different cloak, so to speak, a cut that we prescribe for him. This we must acknowledge as our guilt—and thus will we become sinners who can be justified. . . .

It is not this: Make yourselves great, then you will be proclaiming the Savior to the world. No, no, you pitiful man, die in the blood of Jesus Christ; be humble before all people and especially before God; renounce all arrogance; give yourself over to the hope that you will indeed conquer.

However, it is not *you* who conquers! The only Conqueror in the world is Jesus Christ. We must make way for him; in him we must live and move and have our being. We must stand up for him in repentance, crushed in our own being, sacrificing all that is our own, even the very best that we have. To submit ourselves to him body and soul, with nothing of self remaining — that will assist him to conquer. Truly, dear friends, he is the real Conqueror! Praise God, we know it! He is alive; we know it! The kingdom of God is in his hand; we know it!

THE POOR

The Lord does not forget the cry of the poor.
(Psa. 9:12b; from the German.)

It is a good thing that we have the privilege of being poor. We do not have in mind only the poverty of not knowing how we will be able to make ends meet. That, of course, is a part of it; but it is only secondary. Our truer poverty lies in our effort to achieve what God has in mind for us; it is there that we are indeed most poor.

Many people put all their effort into nonessentials. They concern themselves with things near at hand, seeking to make their own way and arrive at human joy: "Let us eat, drink, and be merry; for tomorrow we die!" It is this situation the Bible calls "being rich." These people, of course, are as poor as anyone. Yet, at least superficially, they are known as rich. In their relation to God, they act as though they are rich. They gobble down every sweet that comes to hand; and when God comes with his nourishment, they are already satisfied; they turn their backs and want nothing.

Strangely enough, it is these poorest of the poor who are called rich; and it is another group who are known as poor. These others have their minds set on something better, something higher; and in their striving they have concluded that ultimately man can be helped only by God himself. When a person arrives at this realization, he has made himself an utter pauper. No self-help here! If everything depends upon God, then it simply does not depend upon us. And the more a person becomes aware that things do not depend upon himself but upon God, the

146

poorer he becomes. And thus the word becomes true: "Blessed are the poor, the poor in spirit, for theirs is the kingdom of Heaven."

It is the cry of these poor ones that the Lord does not forget; these are in fact his people on earth. It is their vocation, so to speak, to receive God and not let themselves be satisfied with anything else. A person in this position is truly poor, because now he has no means of help unless God stands by him. What now is wealth and praise and honor, even health and life? What are these if we have not the person of God as our treasure? All else is worthless. Now one is beggarly poor—and yet rich.

At present, after the world has struggled for thousands of years to become rich, it is not easy to let oneself be numbered among the poor. Yet God always sees to it that there are poor people; and that is of benefit to the development of the kingdom of God. When God finds a noble soul, he creates the circumstances of life that will prevent him from becoming rich. This person does not triumph even in spiritual matters; he cannot say, "I have everything; I know everything."

It follows that someone who is weighed down with a particular burden, who cannot seem to find inner rest, of whom cheerfulness and laughter are not companions—he nevertheless can be quite content. God may be doing a work with him so that he can join the ranks of the poor; his cry may be essential in God's finding a point of contact with mankind. For such a person things often are hard, especially in regard to other people who apparently are doing well. He would like to cry out: "Am I to live in misery, to be counted of no worth among men, to be embarrassed? Am I to be weeping while others make merry? Why does God not give *me* freedom and make me strong?" Indeed, the whole world conspires to convince him that he is a fool if he does not have the same aspirations as others. . . .

So it is no simple and easy matter to be one of the poor and the grieving—and yet this is the very best of situations for us human creatures at the present time. There are today swarms of superficial Christians who wish only to live always on the heights, to feel blessed; but they can't bring it off. Their high lasts only for a time, like intoxication. A person can intoxicate *himself*; he can become intoxicated with the Bible, or with religious practices; he can get himself increasingly impassioned over something and then find that it amounts to nothing at all. None of these things endure.

On the other hand, if people are poor and intent upon complaining about it, we must tell them: "Be content; thank God that you do not belong to the rich, that you are one who has good reason to sigh! Or have you it in mind to forget about God, too? Do your sighing *in faith*, and then you are rich, even when you have cause to sigh."

It is essential that there be people who cry out as though there were no God in the world. Of course, he *is* in the world; but most people are totally separated from him. They go their own ways; and on those ways they go to *ruin*. They carry on all manner of activities that spell godlessness; and thus mankind makes it appear that there is no God in heaven able to work effectively on earth.

Under these circumstances a person certainly has the right to cry out, because a jolly Christianity is the greatest possible folly in a world where millions of brothers and sisters are brought to ruin daily; where murder and killings and deception and cruelty and envy and greed and passion destroy everything; where nations strike out to destroy one another; where people work each other's destruction; where all is dark. In such a world, the cry may well be a vehement one, even to the point of accusing God, "Why have you forsaken us?"

To say that in the right spirit certainly is not unbelief; it is rather a suffering with the world — the world which is, in fact, forsaken by God. Although God loves the world, the world truly is removed from him. And when the poor, amidst everything they already have, yet in faith come to be *hungry* — when they hunger for the nearness of God, hunger for the appearing of the Savior in the final resurrection, hunger for the Holy Spirit who is to be our teacher and guide, hunger precisely for these things *of God* — then they do not commit sin as they cry out.

Even if I possess something which can satisfy me personally but still have this hunger, then I belong to the poor. Nor can it be held against me when I cry out, because the poverty of the world is so great and the general deprivation of mankind is so pressing. Thus the most gifted people, those most richly endowed, can truly come to be reckoned among the poor. The Savior himself joined the poor; and certainly he was rich with the gifts of God. Yet ultimately he was the poorest of the poor and was forced to cry out, "My God, why have you forsaken me?"

In this cry lies our way to God and God's way to us. But as long as we still have some little resource of our own which, under the circumstances, can satisfy us, then we do not break through to the kingdom of heaven, to the power of the kingdom of heaven which is required for the overcoming of the world. A little bit of the kingdom of heaven will not overcome the world. A merely general providence over mankind will not overcome the world. No, it is through the poor that the direct and total rule of God must be drawn into the world in order to overcome it. . . .

So, we must be poor, because it is precisely through our poverty that we are rich. We, apparently unfortunate, are yet in fact richly blessed, because the influence of the poor of the world is greater in its effect than the influence of the greatest kings and emperors. It is precisely through these poor that God's own kingship is drawn to earth.

GOD'S SHEEP

As a shepherd seeks out his flock when some of his sheep have been scattered abroad, so will I seek out my sheep.

(Ezek. 34:12)

Expressions similar to this one from Ezekiel appear frequently in the holy scripture; and these words contain the great thought of God which must be heard and understood among men. The thought of God always is this: No one is to remain lost. Everything that we would call lost is regarded by God as his possession.

With Abraham and even earlier, nothing was ever given up. It is not as though God settled for Abraham when Abraham believed in him. Certainly not! Always, God sees beyond Abraham — and at Abraham's expense! Abraham is not to gain at the expense of the world; but Abraham is to suffer for the benefit of the world. At Abraham's expense, God looks toward all the generations of earth. Israel is called, not that God might have a people in which he can take pleasure, but that through this people he might reach the nations, the masses of mankind which are his sheep. At Israel's expense, God goes out to the nations. And in this same great thought of God, Jesus Christ enters the world, coming into the flesh. It is not that God will settle for a dear Son and a few disciples serving him. No, at the expense of Jesus and his disciples, God is again looking to the nations. Jesus himself says: "I have other sheep, too; they are not of this fold. And I will go out and fetch them; and when I am lifted up, I will draw them all to myself." At Jesus' expense, God is going out to the nations; at the church's expense, the world is to be blessed.

150

In this economy of the kingdom of God it becomes clear what *our* calling is, if we, like Abraham and the prophets, wish to be servants of God in Jesus Christ, to be light in the world. God does not clothe his beloved Christians in velvet and silk and make them blessed in preference to other people; rather, at the expense of his disciples, God wants to make others blessed. We must submit ourselves to God so that we can be, so to speak, God's reserve force when he goes out to look for his sheep. We must stand as pillars; and, as with our Lord and Master, Jesus Christ, we must not falter or waver when, at our expense, God moves out to the nations, to the lost and rejected.

This solidity must be evident in the genuine disciples of Jesus if God is to depend upon them. But such firmness is rare, because we pillars wobble when the demand is made of us: "Give up your body and your life, your possessions and blood, for this cause of God. Do not seek your own interests; but consider, rather, that you will be last to receive the benefits. Only when the others have received the blessing will you receive it."

We who, in Jesus, constitute a people of God must not seek rest until God has found rest, until the lost have been found. You understand now why the work of God does not progress as rapidly as it might; there are not enough people at whose expense God can operate. Man's egoism is too great; and this egoism has corrupted our very faith in God. People seek their own interests in God and thereby lose the character of the fighter and the pillar. They waver; and God has, so to speak, no support.

They waver in a twofold way. They waver in the sense of murmuring when things go ill with them, when it is demanded that they give up their life so that the love of God can reach others, when they are to become a sacrifice for the cause of God. They do not understand what it means to die in the name of God, for the victory of the kingdom of God. It often seems strange to me that people do not understand this. They gladly die for their fatherland; why then do Christians not want to die for their own cause, for the will of God, for the Father of nations? If men of the world can die for their fatherland, why can we not die for the Father? I have often wondered why it is precisely the Christians who become the most egoistic of people. . . .

On grounds of the blood of Jesus Christ, people boast of their own salvation. This is bad! If the blood of Jesus Christ is upon you, then you can claim nothing other than that your life belongs to God and that the lost are to be saved at your expense. The blood of Jesus Christ means that it will cost us our life that the kingdom of God might come. We must not waver, we must not even blink our eyes, when we suffer some loss because of our commitment to the kingdom — even if this means total loss and the giving up of life itself.

But people who should be pillars waver also for another reason: they do not love. They are asked to allow others to share their place with them, and this annoys them; they cannot imagine that someone else is to be their equal. They pass sentence and condemn; they judge and decree condemnation for the world, which they regard as odious. . . . One must have a certain reputation, a certain status in the world, a certain rank, in order to be recognized. We are always intent upon surrounding ourselves with those who have this recognition. We never get near those who are rejected; we ignore them, they are of little concern to us. . . .

Yet neither sin nor devil nor hell carries weight; only man has value. Why, then, do you who are devout condemn the others? Why do you make it difficult for them? Why do you deny them consideration and love? I am afraid our religious societies will never learn what it means to love as God, in his Son, loved the world. We always assume that we have come to God for our own sake; religious people assume that they must eternally be regarded as the honored ones. Nevertheless, it just possibly could be that the spirits who now are exalted will experience wailing and gnashing of teeth and that those who now are despised by them will experience joy and bliss. . . .

Of course, it is not we who can get to the lost ones; we cannot *seek* them. Let no pastor or missionary imagine that he can; we are not commissioned to do that. There is only one shepherd who can seek the lost, and that is Jesus — and the will of God within him. But we are to constitute God's reserve force on earth; and in this way *he* must be able to reach them. . . . We cannot *seek;* we can only walk among men as those who yield body and life in the service of this will of God that does seek the lost. So don't try so much to change people! You are always working to convert them according to your pattern, to drive them into your institutions; and there they are to be sheep who jump to *your* whip. Do not work so much; but be pillars which do not waver when God is getting to the lost. . . .

I believe that Jesus Christ will come, not from heaven as we suppose, but from *his* heaven. The *Savior's* heaven is there where God has his throne; and his throne is not only in heaven but, as it is written, with the destitute and broken. It is from *this* heaven Jesus will come, from this heaven where millions of people sigh and groan in their distress. And that is my heaven, too. I decline your heaven of bliss; I do not want to enter there. The heaven into which I want to enter, the heaven of my Jesus, is where he gives his blood and life that men may receive help — there where the apparently godless are, the apparently rejected and unbelieving. This is the heaven of Jesus Christ.

It will come as the greatest of surprises when one day the word will be heard: "These were my lowliest ones, and you did not feed them!" Why did you not feed them? We thought they were devils! "They were in prison, and you did not visit them!" Why did you not visit them? We thought they were devils! Now *they* are the lowly ones of God who are languishing in misery; and I say: *There* is the heaven of Jesus Christ, *there* is the God who leaves the ninety-nine righteous ones in the wilderness and seeks the lost sheep.

ZION, THE MOUNTAIN OF PEACE

It shall come to pass in the latter days that the mountain of the house of the Lord shall be established as the highest of the mountains, and shall be raised up above the hills; and peoples shall flow to it, and many nations shall come, and say: "Come, let us go up to the mountain of the Lord, to the house of the God of Jacob; that he may teach us his ways and we may walk in his paths." For out of Zion shall go forth the law, and the word of the Lord from Jerusalem. He shall judge between many peoples, and shall decide for strong nations afar off; and they shall beat their swords into plowshares, and their spears into pruning hooks; nation shall not lift up sword against nation, neither shall they learn war any more. (Mic. 4:1 – 3)

"What is the point of origin for God's supervision of the nations?" We answer: The existence of Zion, the mountain of peace, is the basis of all God's decisions in world history. Not for their own sake, but for the sake of Zion, nations must fall and rise again. "I give peoples in exchange for your life" (Isa. 43:4), God says with reference to the continuance of his Mount Zion.

What then is Zion on earth? We say concisely: Zion is the Savior, Jesus Christ, and what belongs to him. With him is bound up a history on earth in which, in ever widening circles, individual people, whole nations, and ultimately the whole world shall be caught up. The goal of this history is a kingdom of peace based on a new world-order. All of God's utterances through the prophets tell us this. Likewise, all the verdicts of God are manifested in judgment and grace, because, in consequence of these, all nations shall come and worship God (Rev. 15:4).

The faith that this mountain of peace has its triumphal history in Jesus, to the honor of God the Father; and the assurance that, in the interests of total victory, God the Almighty governs not only the church of Christ but all nations as well — these make us happy and confident and allow our hearts to become wide, since through these we become emancipated from paltry jealousy against each other.

Before God, all nations have equal worth; yet, in the course of time, those people are blessed who enter into God's plans with a self-denying love that seeks the good of all nations. The history of Zion, this mountain of peace, is not open for all to see, as is the transitory history of a nation. The stirrings of God's kingdom-history originate in eternity and reach the nations in a variety of juridical sentences; but people seldom see the connection between their moment of history and the sovereign rule of the King of Kings. Yet the person who believes does perceive something of this connection and trembles with longing for progress in the history of Mount Zion.

The word of God which we have in our text intensifies this longing to no end, because it predicts a time when that history no longer will be concealed, when it will be openly manifest before all eyes that Mount Zion (or, let us now say, Jesus and his judgments) alone is immutable and thus can be regarded as the highest good and most desirable goal in all the world.

When God's rule in Christ breaks through into the world, and when the new law of life embodied in Christ becomes dominant, then we shall see the salvation of all creation. In him, all things have life; and that which has died we shall see return to life. In him, too, we shall see the removal of all the evil from among the nations. His disciples experience something of these realities even now. What will it be when *the nations* acknowledge them?

No wonder our text speaks with excitement: "And they shall come and say: Come, let us go up to the mountain of the Lord, that he may teach us his ways." Here the promise is given that Zion's salvation shall become known to the nations. It is not that God shall seek *them;* rather, they shall *seek God* on this Zion, in the name of the Lord Jesus. It will become clear to them that, from here, laws are issued which man needs in order to live, that here is to be found the life-giving word of God which can create a new birth.

When, in coming to the knowledge of Mount Zion, the nations renounce their old ways in order to gain something new, the result will be the beginning of a great age of peace, a rapid transition to a new life upon a new earth under a new heaven. All this, God will accomplish through Mount Zion. Peoples and nations will come under the judgment of Jesus Christ; and he it will be who, in the end, will compel the hearts of the nations. He will do so with a strong hand and stern righteousness — although without forgetting his primary work of *reconciliation.* What shall be well-forgotten are the deeds of the murderer and the liar, the long centuries of bloodletting. We shall recognize one another as God's people, who are called to works of peace, who, together, can again become the crown of creation through our head, Jesus Christ.

As we remember, let us always do so with a view to this great goal of Zion, the mountain of peace, loftier than all the mountains of the world.

THE RIGHTEOUSNESS OF GOD

The righteousness of God through faith in Jesus Christ for all who believe. (Rom. 3:22)

This is a verse that has become utterly distorted in translation. There is no "righteousness before God" in the sense that the righteousness which I acquire through faith has validity before God. Rather, the Bible always says, as it does here, that *God's righteousness* has been revealed through faith in Jesus Christ for all who believe. That is something very different.

I am not to inquire *subjectively* whether I will be justified before God. I am to ask how *God's righteousness* may come upon me — *objectively*. Open your ears, I'll say it again. We are not to ask, "Will I be justified before God?" but rather, "How do I attain the righteousness of God?" The Bible never says, "The righteousness which is valid before God." Luther translated it that way because he had an erroneous idea in his head, and so the Bible had to submit.

The Bible always says "God's righteousness"; and this is achieved through faith, not through the law. Legalism does not achieve God's rightness and truth; but our conduct in faith toward God brings us *God's* righteousness. The world cannot of itself attain this; and you cannot attain it, either. All your effort is in vain. You may struggle all your life to do everything to a "T." You may be as brave and as good as you like. You may found a society which is smooth as a mirror, where people hardly laugh anymore, let alone dance and frequent the bar, and where the daily activity is only rising, praying, working, praying, eating, praying, sleeping, praying. Go ahead and create such a society; the world will not be helped thereby. All your effort to be righteous before God is nothing but a waste of time.

Are you sure that it is not occasionally the righteousness of God to dance? If it pleases God that you dance once in a while, why don't you dance then? Did not David have to dance once for the sake of God? "But I don't approve," you say. There legalism rises against righteousness, and legalism strikes the deathblow.

Can the righteousness of God still get a hearing in the churches today? No, the righteousness of God has to adjust itself to the church's legalism. We stray into superstition and bad habits, because we seek *our* righteousness before God; and that is wrong. You are not to be righteous; God wants to be righteous. You are not to seek what would be your own righteousness. You can't succeed; that doesn't amount to anything. What do you think you can do that would in any way honor God? Your concern should be that God's righteousness enter the world.

This can happen when you offer yourself to Christ and say, "It is not I who live; Christ is to live; the righteousness of God comes through *him*." And God's righteousness can be revealed in you just as you are. You can exemplify the righteousness of God even while you are sick; therefore, rejoice! You can exemplify the righteousness of God while you are in temptation and distress; therefore, rejoice! God wants only for you to allow him to be at work in *his* righteousness.

There is a purpose of God in our having to endure struggle. It makes no difference if we feel ourselves to be sinners, as long as we know that God is dealing with us as he chooses. We must not seek ourselves and our righteousness; we must seek to have God enter into the world with his righteousness. And when he says that, with his coming, we will see ourselves all the more as sinners, then we must rejoice and gladly acknowledge ourselves to be such, if only God comes with his light. Though I may be black as coal, yet I know that, when the light of the righteousness of God comes, I may well be burned but I nevertheless will arise anew in the righteousness of God.

Yet this objectivity has been utterly lost in Christianity. "I want to stand before God — I, I, I!" Oh, you poor man, don't worry about your standing before God; but see to it that God and his righteousness can get to you whether you stand or not! And if he must strike you down, rejoice, because you will rise again afterwards. But your first concern should be not that you gain something but that God does. . . .

Submit yourself so that the righteousness of God can jolt and shake you. Do not seek to be reckoned righteous; that would be at least partially deception, as though God were to say: "It doesn't matter even if you are not properly clean; I won't look too carefully. Just believe that you are credited with being righteous." No, the righteousness of God must get into the world in an *honest* fashion; otherwise all Christianity is useless!

What kind of a world do we have? A Christian world? Yes; but one full of unrighteousness! Yet God wants to dwell with us; he wants us to make a way so that he personally can rule in every heart. For this reason Jesus died and has said, "Die with me so that our God may come, so that his righteousness may come upon earth." Rejoice, then, when everything is destroyed. When body and soul suffer pain and are in trouble, rejoice! The righteousness of God must be revealed in all flesh.

But when that which *God* calls "righteous" is revealed, then you will be surprised. We don't anymore know what is right and pleasing to God. Actually, only one thing pleases him — and that is when he sees that I am not pleased with myself, when I say that I, with all my house, want to be broken in pieces because no part of me is wholly right. This attitude alone sustains me! In nothing that we carry on here — whether eating and drinking, sleeping or working — is there yet righteousness. We still can't do anything right. We still have not been able enough to make a way for God; and, consequently, we are perplexed in many matters.

And yet, finally, the world must be saved through righteousness and judgment. So we must crucify ourselves and exert effort; and perhaps then God's righteousness will yet be revealed—whether in judgment or in kindness, either way will suit me fine. We dare not stand up to face the nations before this righteousness has been established. A preaching of the gospel behind which there is nothing but unrighteousness has very little value.

We don't even know, for example, whether God approves our sitting in church. When you have worked all week and are tired, then, under certain circumstances, it may be right for you to stay in bed—and it may be a disgrace to God when you place your broken body on the hard church pew. God wants to lead us according to the truth of life; and our best may be despised by him because there is falsehood in it. He may indeed say, "Get away from me with your bawling; seek righteousness and not legalism." . . .

It is terribly discouraging that one little word could have caused such confusion for centuries. Because Luther said, "I seek my righteousness in faith," the entire Lutheran Church has adopted a wrong course. I do not want to force this idea onto people; they wouldn't understand it anyway. But I, personally, want to make an about-face; and I hope that, if I accomplish it, God can deal with me in such way that something comes out of it that will serve others as well.

We must sacrifice ourselves for the righteousness of God. Forget about yourself. Don't always seek to be right in yourself; pray only that God may come. He will jolt you, of course; and the deepest motives of your being will be exposed; and these things cannot occur without much bitter pain. But let us rejoice even when the way leads through the severest judgments. Let us rejoice in the judgments, because we do not want to become happy with our sins, but we want God to rejoice in his creation; and we do not wish to stand between him and his creation any longer. Only in this way do we serve God aright; and then he can use us once more.

WONDERS

*In your majesty ride forth victoriously for the cause of truth
and to defend the right; and let your right hand perform wonders.*
(Psa. 45:4; second part from the German.)

This we know for certain: if the Lord once should draw the line in this world according to truth and right, then wonders would have to come crashing in upon one another, because at the same time, that which has become crooked would have to be broken and straightened out. Things will not straighten out on their own. They have become so accustomed to being crooked that they will have to be broken, as when a doctor breaks a limb that has grown crooked in order to straighten it out. The doctor is harsh and must use force; but when God rides forth for the cause of truth, things go more easily, because he does not use force; he uses *wonders*. He enables things to become normal again, so that the perverted is made right and the crooked straight —and, with that, a "wonder" has occurred.

These wonders of God always come in connection with truth, in connection with the right. Consequently, they are never marvels which astound and leave us confused as to what their meaning might be. Always light is produced; always things make sense; always the event has moral value. Therefore, we do not really have to beg for *wonders*; we need simply pray: "Dear God, be so kind as to draw the line according to truth in our house! Work according to the right among us, that is, in the hearts that are here. Dispense with ceremonies, and move straight ahead!"

Then there will be no lack of wonders. Wherever it is needed, things will be made right; and there will not be cause for a great commotion about it. If difficult matters present themselves, or if you get into a very perplexing situation and don't know which way to turn, don't just catch hold of the situation at the point where its awkwardness is apparent and seek to heal it from there. That awkwardness one must bear and suffer. But look behind, where something is not right, and say to God, "Make that right! Here is something of falsehood, and there; I can't remove it; you will have to do it!" Then the wounds will heal; and the awkwardness on the outward side of life will fall away when inwardly matters are established according to the truth.

We have no inkling of how much falsehood there is inside man, how much self-deception, how much self-conceit, how much ill will, how many deaf ears. And all this can be so cunningly hidden, while outwardly one appears quite polished. A whole society can appear to be very elegant, while underneath it amounts to nothing. This is the cause of many maladies, because one trouble leads to others. Physical deformity is a result of the deformity and distortion in the inner part of mankind and of the individual. Of course, it is not as though the distress of the individual — say, his physical illness — is necessarily the direct result of *his own* inner perversion. No, everything is intertwined. We are like a chain in which the corporate deformity produces its fruits right along with those of individual deformity, to the point that we cannot determine from where this or that stems. We can only say that, in general, if things were operating closer to truth and right, matters would be very different. Therefore, we don't pray, "Do wonders!" but rather, "Let truth prevail! Let things be broken so that they can be set right!" Ask this, and we don't need to concern ourselves about the rest.

This verse is a real encouragement for me, because recently I have had great trouble concerning the wonders being performed nowadays. Often I am asked what one should make of them. Through Spiritism, Magnetism, and the like, men perform the greatest wonders, healing everything. And the whole business is *Christian!* They say:

We all believe in one true God,
Jew, Christian, Turk, and Hottentot.

There are stories, too, of the immediate effectiveness of the laying on of hands. People are struck with astonishment. Yet these all are *oddities* and not *wonders*; they are not bound up with some truth. Assume for the moment that one of these people were able to heal all the sick at one blow; what would we have gained? Then we could jump about for a little while, until we got sick again! Beyond that, nothing would have been achieved.

I am saying this only to make you cautious. God shall perform wonders, true — yet only if they grow from the setting right of the inner man. There must be a basis, a kingdom-basis, from which we are illumined and renewed in our godly aspects. It is there that the wonders shall take place; and then we can shout for joy when outward things become right because of what has happened inside.

However, then the significance of outward wonders diminishes; one does not speak so much of the healing of the body. This wanting to heal from the outside inwards makes me very suspicious of all such phenomena; and I would like to draw your attention to it. Spiritism can cure; Magnetism can cure; Sorcery can cure; and now prayer can cure, too — everything can cure. Everyone wants help in the area of medicine. Yet they want only to be healed; they have no interest in God! And it is strange that, in these stories of healing, it always is added, "So and so many doctors have confirmed it!" — as though it were necessary for the doctors to confirm God!

I am quick to say for the sake of *our* house: I am sorry that we have acquired a reputation of healing and have been placed on a plane with so-called Prayer-Cure Institutions. Yet anyone who has been with us for a while must certainly be aware that this is not what we are after. I do not want to see a single miracle performed upon anyone which is not the consequence of the inner righting of that person. I would be afraid for the person who got well so quickly. He would deceive himself if he supposed that he were something now that his little finger had been healed. He would be spiritually deceived!

"Therefore, O Lord, ride forth for the cause of truth! Make hearts right! Let the inner man become something genuine and proper!" And then what can and must take place in the outward man will happen of itself.

NEVERTHELESS I WILL HOLD TO THEE

Nevertheless I will hold to thee; thou dost hold my right hand. Thou dost guide me with thy counsel, and afterward thou wilt receive me to glory. Whom have I in heaven but thee? And there is nothing upon earth that I desire besides thee. My flesh and my heart may fail, but God is the strength of my heart and my portion for ever. (Psa. 73:23 – 26; first line from the German.)

The subject of this passage is God, whom very few people understand. When we read such words, we must consider how the Psalmist was able to say: "Nevertheless I will hold to thee."

In what way do I *have* him? Is God something one can grasp? Can one lay hold of him with the hands? If a strong man is standing at my side and I am in danger of falling, I hold on to him; then I can say: "If only I have you, then I will not fall." But what then is God?

In our misery we have made it a habit to say, "God! God! God!" But with very few people is there any substance behind the cry, because, when God does something rather different from what they expected, they fall anyway and remain down until some other person comes and helps them up. Thus there is a whole flood of terminology with which these people satisfy themselves, because it is part of social etiquette in our day to be just a little pious. But when life comes to the point where "their flesh and their heart may fail," then they despair: "No, I cannot bear to have my soul fail, or I am undone!"

Or if heaven and earth tremble, if my fate on earth becomes uncomfortable or difficult, brings conflict or heartache, then to what shall I hold? Where is my God then?

When we read the scriptures, we are always amazed at how firm a stand those people were able to take. We must consider, however, that in Israel they did not speak of God in the giddy way we do. When they spoke of God they thought of him in relation to something, something established upon earth; and it was to that they fastened themselves. When, therefore, the author of this psalm said, "Nevertheless I will hold to thee always! . . . if I have only thee! . . . thou art my God!" he was thinking of something he had *experienced* — and that was God. Consequently, the Israelites called God "Yahweh" — meaning "he who has so given himself as to be experienced," he of whom it can be said: "There he is! Lay hold of him!" That is what the word "Yahweh" means: "There he is!" And with him I will remain, where *he* is.

And where was he? He was with Abraham and began something there. He was with Isaac and continued there. He was with Jacob and made further progress there. He was with Joseph, with Moses, and there proved himself the one who *acts*, out of whose deeds a people emerged, a people presenting itself time and again as a *saved* people.

Following these accomplished deeds, the *promises* of God appeared. As he has done once, so he will do again. And his history is eternal, for God is with us. He has begun a work; and he will bring it to completion!

Thus the biblical people reminded themselves of the history that lay behind them — not merely their national history, but also the life-history that lay behind each one. Their personal history fell into place as a part of world history, as part of their national history. Read the hymn of praise that Mary sang, or the thanksgiving hymn of Hannah or Deborah, or the many psalms that people of this sort sang. All of them were people of the world who in their own lot were *experiencing* the great story of God in the world.

At times things went against them, and it seemed as though they had fallen prey to destruction; but then they rose, and there they were again! In this up-and-down of events, of individual fortunes and those of the nation, they observed God; they saw how God steps in to act. Out of these many experiences an image of God was formed in the hearts and emotions of the Israelites. They never philosophized about God as we do; a Jew would have been ashamed to do that!

But we have carried on for thousands of years now — and one stupidity follows another. We lose the vision of what God already is in us and what of him already has become history in us — and then we are unable to endure hardship. Poor rogues that we are, we immediately suffer defeat and give up in despair: "Where then is God?" We see only outward things; and according to how these affairs are going, we are either contented or we are not. And thus God, the living God, the God who reveals himself, of whom one can say, "There he is!" does not acquire a people; and man loses the ground under his feet. . . .

We must come to the point where we can experience God again and in that experience have fellowship with him. I am not talking about any sort of theology; something much more real than *words* must enter our being! There must be *deeds*! Deeds are true, and on them one can stand secure. By them, we regularly can observe, in our own lives or in the lives of others, that God has begun a work! . . . We must have in mind something specific. Thus, we keep insisting that something be *experienced*. You must consider *talk* as something quite secondary. Others may instruct all they wish; we want *experience*. And, praise God, not only do we want it, but we actually get it.

Frequently I experience something, so that, in my room, I am compelled to fall down on my face in thankfulness and worship before God and say, "Praise and thanks be to God, that person is now saved for eternity!" The person himself, of course, is jubilant and happy too; yet, often he does not know what a great thing he has experienced. If tomorrow something unpleasant comes along, he is laid low, whimpering. It is as though he had been given a mere penny, so readily he throws away his experience!

We must acquire wisdom. We must get to the place where,

if for decades we experience nothing and it seems as though God is leading us through a tunnel, we keep reminding ourselves that once we did stand in the sun. If there were nothing to experience and one were forced back upon "spiritual uplift," I would have nothing to say; such hours of inspiration pass away. If we had only spiritual inspiration to depend upon, then we would be the most miserable people on earth.

But do not be unduly anxious; God gives to his children as they sleep. Just keep your heart in the right place and remain inwardly attentive. When an action of God does take place, then open your eyes! In that way, a person can experience something, whether it be in the spirit (in which case the experience is adapted to your total being and remains perfectly natural) or whether it be in the physical life. But one can experience something if he wishes to. Even if one does not desire experience, he may get it nonetheless; but he will not perceive it. One could even be very pious in all this; but he would not then understand the words of our psalm.

If we stand within the kingdom of God, we must expect his action in history. We can observe God in world history today, too. In the whole world we can see something of the rule of God and can say, "No human being did *that!*" But a person is not an accurate observer if he sees the world only from the perspective of his own partisan viewpoint; that which is of God cannot then be seen.

One cannot imagine a newspaper today that would be like the books of the Kings, observing and judging the history of Germany according to good or evil. With us, it is the custom to distinguish between Frenchmen and Germans, between nobility and peasants, between various social strata and religions, but not between good and evil. In that regard, we give no verdict! We would have mankind divided between church-goers and non-church-goers; but this distinction is not to be found in the Bible. That is why the Bible is so refreshing — it makes a distinction only between good and evil.

If we have eyes to see, then the good and the evil will be

distinguished for us as well. Then we will be able to see where in history God is and where he is not. Then we will have God materially among us on earth. Take a look into life where you live and into the people round about you; when once you observe something, then hold to it; and though body and soul may languish, do not be whining and weeping any longer!

Many people believe that, if once they come under the rule of God, their lives must of necessity be free from instability and turmoil. That is totally wrong. It is precisely when you have come to God that life becomes threatening, because it is only then that you are in fact alive and able to endure anything at all. Previously you could endure nothing. But if once you have experienced something from God, then you are able to pass through tribulation; and your tribulation will produce fruit. Others cannot endure it; but we can endure even death and not be fearful; we can endure hell itself and be unafraid.

God needs to have one of his children in every hell, because it is only through them that he can enter that hell in order to bring it to an end. Therefore, we must enter into all tribulation and endure in it, carrying the comfort of God with us into it, even into hell itself. Thus we are to be present as a people of comfort, a living gospel.

If no man of comfort were willing to enter into hell, that would be terrible indeed. Jesus was a man of comfort upon earth and in hell, in the desert and in palaces, at the side of sinners and of the righteous. He could endure all things, for his Father was in him and was his life. And so he says to us, "Endure it, for what you endure with me, you endure with God; and with us nothing is in vain."

The most insignificant event must serve for good, must bear fruit. Just so, the least significant human being can come to have worth in heaven and on earth. Zacharias and his wife, through their firmness, could contribute to the birth of John the Baptist; and Mary could become the mother of the Savior.

To want to endure nothing is great foolishness; to believe that you are forsaken by God if you must endure something is one of the silliest concepts among those belonging to the kingdom of God. For if the kingdom of God lays hold on us, where do you think God is going to go with us? Clearly, we remain within this foolish world; we cannot live in heaven but must remain below in the dirt. We are impelled to move into all the situations in which people exist. We must pass through all the grief that other people have, because there is to be a man of faith in every sorrow of the world.

Thus, we must enter into these things, perhaps for long periods of time. Perhaps we must endure to the point that we hear and see nothing of God, until finally God, who is with us in the distress, can bring light into the situation. The very fact that God is in it with us means that the matter cannot fail; ultimately God comes to be acknowledged in every tribulation. But we are impelled to enter into it; he must have us, because he wishes to be a God of people, not a philosophical concept. He wants to have children who remain alive even in the deepest darkness. In this way the kingdom of God will finally come.

Many would be quite content if the kingdom were to come *to them*; but they will have to wait a long time, because that is not the way it works. Rather, God sends his own into the world; they are to be his gospel! In this way we must *endure*, until the whole world is filled with his living gospel. God grant that in this way we might become servants and bear our tribulation.

However, never should we permit the tribulation to come *into our hearts*! Do not permit the satan of sadness to enter. Away with this satan! If it becomes dark in your heart, you can no longer be a person who bears fruit. Today, everyone is called upon to be a living gospel to the glory of God — the God who is with us in the deepest tribulation and darkness and who leads us out again to the high places of life.

THE POWER OF GOD

"Because the poor are despoiled, because the needy groan,
I will now arise," says the Lord, "and I will bring relief."
(Psa. 12:5; last part from the German.)

How? How does God do it? That is always a puzzle. Everywhere in the Bible we find this: "Get away, let me do it." Sometimes, of course, it sounds as though God is lamenting, as though he were not quite able; but then comes a time when he says, "I can too! The poor are before me, and I must help them." But how?

Different answers are given. The faint-hearted say, "Yes, he knows how to bless even in distress; and then, of course, there is eternity beyond." But in this way not one single misery comes to an end; not one solitary tear is dried! And this is how this business of eternity is; let's face it honestly: If I am constantly advised to seek comfort *in eternity*, then I cannot genuinely trust God. If I see nothing of succor in this world, who can guarantee it for the next? Or did the Savior come only into the beyond? It seems to me he came *to us*!

Consequently, comfort cannot simply be equated with "the beyond." Even if in some temporal situations the outcome is not restricted to this earthly life but lies beyond it, the question still remains whether that outcome will be attained immediately upon my leaving this life. I don't believe it will. God does not operate in the world in so mechanical a way. Matters run much more naturally; and the struggle is more difficult than we imagine. One cannot simply be jumping around in the world and then die—and expect that matters are settled for all eternity. Rather, there are developments; there is progress or regression to the degree that the distress can be taken from us and God can succeed in giving relief.

Our achieving blessedness is a question of the power of God. He must employ force, and it is for us to have faith in his capability. After all, God has made us! When, in their spirits, people come near this power of God, they always draw a little of it into themselves and thereby become the best possible instruments of God, in that they have drawn from him a portion of his ministering power.

It is not so much a matter of a person making an obvious and sudden change toward conversion; of primary importance is the fact that God bestirs himself on that person's behalf and gathers him in. The history of our redemption progresses by moments of God's demonstrating his aid, in acts toward which we can contribute nothing. And some day, when we shall be in the kingdom of heaven and when the last shock, the jolt of death, has come, we will look back once more and marvel at how often God had to intervene powerfully on our behalf, even against our will, in order that we might be saved. God's action on our behalf always takes this form: he is in heaven and keeps approaching us, pressing in on us, until he can enter our life here in this world.

This is the intent of God's effort toward us. And consequently, our assistance regularly seems delayed. Our distress is not alleviated until the barrier of eternity, between this life and the beyond, is penetrated. The opening must be made *from above*, not from down here upwards. Christendom has gotten this reversed; now we would make many openings *up*, out of the world. Through these we would fly like the doves and be saved; and yet we don't even know what is out there! Some people even want to hurry death along; but when they get across to the other side, they make big eyes! One must be extremely cautious! It is very painful for me that the truth of this reversal can't get through to the mind of Christendom. This is why Christianity functions so poorly.

I know how "Blumhardtian" all this is. People will say, "Now

Blumhardt is coming up with his queer stories again." But I wish you would prove to me which is biblical: our going to God in death, or God's coming to us in life. From the first to the last chapter, the Bible deals with God's coming into the world; and of all this business about dying, nothing is said.

Every word in the Bible guarantees for me God's action *here*, where I now stand. If God raises only one finger against my distress, more is accomplished than if men organize a hundred thousand benevolent institutions. It is God's action we need; and very quickly God will have to do something for us, because we cannot pull the load. We must ask God to bestir himself; and we must become *biblical* again. I would like to say nothing but this: Become biblical! This is what produces understanding and wisdom: our maintaining as a priority the truth that God comes down and Jesus comes down, and that we claim our privilege *on earth*. Sin and death are overcome *here*, not through our faith, but through the power of God.

Our pitiful faith doesn't accomplish anything anyway. Most people merely believe according to their heads. This sounds harsh; but I can't help it. I can't bear such prattle about "faith," because it produces the most self-loving of people. They pay attention only to themselves. I, too, know what faith is. But a faith which *we* create, in which we wish to see things go according to our own ideas, such a faith I don't want. The power of God saves us; and that power is obliged to save many people who don't even believe aright. Who among us would stand up with his faith and say, "Look, I have the right faith!"? That is delusion! But when we reverse this thing and make it biblical, then light comes into every situation, we acquire totally different hearts and heads, totally different hands and feet.

We must be constantly mindful of God's efforts to come into the world and achieve something *here*. We must not be satisfied merely to have a religion, as the heathen have a religion, even if a little different. God puts no store by our religion. When he finds it impossible to come down and help people, he prefers to permit them to become irreligious. In Egypt, the children of

Israel were allowed to do as they pleased, and they became religiously dissipated. But God undertook their cause anyway, because his help does not depend on religion but on his own faithfulness and mercy and power and on the hearts that wait for him to come down.

In this we want to be united, in this hope and in the assurance that God sees the destitute on earth and then says, "There, now I will arise; now I will do it and bring relief." And we know that on the day of Jesus Christ a great restitution is yet to come!

THE RIGHT GOD

Know therefore that the Lord your God is God, the faithful God who keeps covenant and steadfast love with those who love him and keep his commandments, to a thousand generations.

(Deut. 7:9)

A person must know whether his faith is on the right track or not. I think that many people gradually become unbelievers because, of course, they don't have the right God. In the course of time, Christendom has dropped the right God and acquired a philosophical God—still under the name of the old faith but without the actual reality. The true reality has slipped away. One thinks of God simply as someone in the upper spheres who does not manifest himself to us in our circles as a God of action. . . .

No wonder so many folks become unbelievers! I wouldn't believe in such a God either. "If that which you are preaching to me is God, then I am through; then I will not become a pastor!" This was my sentiment even when I was at the university. "You have the same words, but you no longer have the thing itself. You postulate a God without hands, without a mouth, without feet—so that we can simply do as we please. God has to keep his mouth shut and is prohibited from doing anything." No thanks, I won't believe in such a God!

The same holds true for Christ. When anyone speaks of demon possession, people turn green with rage. They say that the Savior was deluded, that those were notions of the time, that we don't need that sort of thing today because we have doctors and hospitals, and that is all we need. . . .

But then they can dispute very nimbly about the deity of

Christ and speak of how he was God's Son — so that one way or another, we are deprived of a Savior *on earth*. Yet I tell you, the Savior doesn't ask what we think of his deity or his humanity; he inquires only whether we want to make use of him or not. We weren't commissioned to ponder his person. Whatever he may have been we shall discover soon enough in heaven. But to us it is said: "He is your Savior! Do you want him, or don't you? May he do something for you, or may he not? Are you going to throw him out as the Pharisees did, or do you want to have him as the tax collectors did?" . . .

It often may seem that God doesn't do anything, no matter how much we beg. In this or that area of life it is as though everything has gone dead. What is the consequence? That we say, as many do, "Now I believe nothing anymore!"? No, rather I say, "Then we don't have *him*. We have gotten onto a wrong track; we are no longer turned to him in the right way, because only a God who intervenes is our God. If he does nothing, it is not our God."

But, take notice! When you again get pointed right, then you have his faithfulness again, you have his mercy again, then something must happen again. Then we can stand up again and say, "That is our God!"

We shall never again be able to convince the world with preaching or with books. The world today will have nothing to do with fantasies. For devout people these are fine; but our world of machines and commerce and life, where people seek a solid foundation on which they can stand, this entire world of business which laughs at us when we come with our ideas — people of *this* world will no longer decide in favor of a religion of fantasy. . . .

We don't need a religion; we need a man, a God. And if we don't get a God, what then is the purpose of all our Christianity? It produces hypocrites! It is as dynamic as cobblestones are! We need an action-God, a God who *does* something. That is the God of the Bible. The rest will come of itself.

That is what Israel had with its Yahweh. There it was said, "That is the right God! Didn't you see the smoke on Sinai? Didn't you hear his voice and the trumpets? Didn't you notice how he gives bread and water when these are lacking, and how he led you with a wonderful hand? Remember that! That is your God; he is the right God; he is able. The other gods are nothing; they have mouths and do not speak, they have hands and do not grasp, they have feet and do not run. But your God is the right God."

And thus it must be with us in regard to the man Jesus. The Lord Jesus is able; and when he does something, then we can say: "Behold, that is the right God; he is able. Your theological prattle means nothing to me." . . . We can no longer manage with words alone; there must be *deeds*. "Save us! Save us! Help us, O faithful God, and *do* something!" And then, when salvation comes, then there is light. . . .

Know that the Lord, your God, who demonstrates himself to you and performs deeds, he is the right God. He is the God who made heaven and earth. He is a faithful God who leads his cause on to the end. Let us place our hope in him today. Let us together cry and pray, "Lord, *do* something for the many, many people!" And our cry will not be in vain; we shall yet experience it. As I have said, much is tossed down from heaven to those who cry out. He feeds the hungry ravens; and he will not let his children pray in vain!

APPENDIX

Ragaz made no effort to identify sources for any of the Blumhardt quotations he used; so we can be of no help regarding the items of Part One.

Regehr made his selections from the four-volume collection of the works of the younger Blumhardt, *Christoph Blumhardt: Eine Auswahl aus seinen Predigten, Andachten und Schriften* [CFBL], herausgegeben von R. Lejeune (Rotapfel Verlag, 1925–37). The location and origins of the items of Part Two are as per the following table:

"THE NAME JESUS"
CFBL, I, #12, pp. 50–63. Sermon preached New Year's Day, 1883; published in *Briefblaetter aus Bad Boll.* (highly abridged)

"ALL THINGS NEW"
CFBL, IV, #9, pp. 71–76. Evening worship of September 18, 1909. (abridged)

"IN THE RETURN OF JESUS CHRIST"
CFBL, IV, #28, pp. 230–38. Sermon preached October 29, 1911. (very highly condensed)

"WAIT FOR THE LORD"
CFBL, I, #9, pp. 32–38. First part preached January 22, 1882, the second on January 3, 1882; appeared as a unit in *Briefblaetter aus Bad Boll*, February 15, 1882. (abridged)

"STANDING BEFORE THE SON OF MAN"
CFBL, II, #6, pp. 74–86. From a stenographic copy; a sermon preached November 25, 1888, at the close of the church year. (highly condensed)

"GOD SO LOVED THE WORLD"
CFBL, III, #5, pp. 33–40. Preached on Pentecost Sunday, June 7, 1897.

"WHO FORGIVES ALL YOUR INIQUITY"
CFBL, I, #21, pp. 103–108. Published table talk of January 11, 1884. (the last half)

"TRUE REPENTANCE"
CFBL, II, #38, pp. 279–88. From a stenographic copy; a sermon preached August 9, 1891. (very much condensed)

"THE POOR"
CFBL, III, #19, pp. 130–37. Table talk of April 25, 1898. (first half)

"GOD'S SHEEP"
CFBL, III, #46, pp. 315–22. Published table talk of June 10, 1899. (abridged)

"ZION, THE MOUNTAIN OF PEACE"
CFBL, I, #39, pp. 199–202. Written for the commemoration of the Franco-German War of 1870 and published in *Stuttgarten Evangelisches Sonntagsblatt*, August 30, 1885. (second half)

"THE RIGHTEOUSNESS OF GOD"
CFBL, II, #57, pp. 434–38. From a stenographic copy; table talk of September 28, 1893. (slightly condensed)

"WONDERS"
CFBL, I, #46, pp. 230–33. First part of the table talk of January 30, 1886; published. (abridged)

"NEVERTHELESS I WILL HOLD TO THEE"
CFBL, III, #14, pp. 98–103. Evening Bible study of January 8, 1898.

"THE POWER OF GOD"
CFBL, I, #49, pp. 239–44. Table talk of February 12, 1886; from a stenographic copy. (first part)

"THE RIGHT GOD"
CFBL, I, #78, pp. 420–24. Table talk of September 24, 1887; from a stenographic copy. (condensed)